PROGRESS MONITORING ASSESSMENT

DRA2®

Developmental Reading Assessment®

Joetta M. Beaver and Mark A. Carter, Ph.D.

PEARSON

Acknowledgments

The authors of the *DRA®2 Progress Monitoring Assessments* would like to thank all of the classroom teachers and reading specialists who participated in field tests for these assessments and provided us with valuable feedback and suggestions for improvement.

PEARSON

ISBN-13: 978-1-4284-2307-7
ISBN-10:   1-4284-2307-9
10 V011 15 14

CONTENTS

Progress Monitoring Assessment CD-ROM

The CD-ROM provides all the reproducible assessments needed for monitoring the progress of your Tier 2 and Tier 3 students throughout the year. *DRA2 Progress Monitoring Assessment* covers oral reading fluency, comprehension, vocabulary, and word reading.

- 95 one-page Student Passages for Levels 4 through 60
- Teacher Observation Guide for each assessment
- Recording forms for tracking students' performance
- Graphic organizers and Sound-Spelling Cards for follow-up instruction

Progress Monitoring Assessment Teacher Guide

The *Teacher Guide* includes

- An overview of *DRA2 Progress Monitoring Assessment*
- Guidelines for administering the assessments and analyzing students' performance
- Moving into Instruction recommendations for every skill assessed with each Student Passage
- Reproducible graphic organizers for follow-up instruction

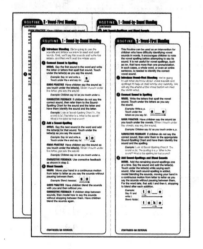

Instructional Routine Cards

This set of sixteen routines provides explicit instructional strategies for teaching and practicing fluency, retelling, summarizing, vocabulary, and word reading.

Also available

EDL2 Evaluación para verificar el progreso

Joetta M. Beaver

Joetta Beaver has worked in the field of education for more than thirty years. She has held various educational positions, including classroom teacher (Grades K–5), reading teacher (Grades 2–6), Reading Recovery teacher leader, Grades K–5 Language Arts and Assessment coordinator, and Early Education teacher-leader. Joetta has served as Vice President and President of the Board of Directors of the Reading Recovery Council of North America.

Joetta received both her Bachelor of Science in Elementary Education and Master's Degree in Reading from Ohio State University in Columbus, Ohio. She has conducted in-service training and presented at a variety of conferences throughout the United States and Canada on topics such as Using Assessments to Drive Instruction, Supporting Emergent Readers and Writers in the Classroom, and Changes over Time in Reading and Writing. Joetta is the primary author of the *Developmental Reading Assessment® (DRA2) Grades K–3* and the *DRA Word Analysis*. She is the co-author of the *Developing Writer's Assessment (DWA) Grades K–6* and the *Developmental Reading Assessment (DRA2) Grades 4–8*.

Mark C. Carter, Ph.D.

Mark C. Carter has been an educator for more than thirty years, holding the positions of elementary classroom teacher (Grades 2–6), Elementary Instructional Specialist, and coordinator of Grades K–12 Assessment for Language Arts and Mathematics. Currently Mark teaches middle school language arts in Ohio.

Mark received his Master's Degree from Ohio State University in 1978. He completed the requirements for his Ph.D. in Early and Middle Childhood Education in 1992 and received his doctorate degree from Ohio State University. Mark earned National Board Certification in 2002 as a Middle Childhood Teacher. Dr. Carter does in-service training throughout the United States, continues to teach graduate courses, and writes extensively about classroom-based assessment practices. He is co-author of the *Portfolio Assessment in the Reading and Writing Classroom*, the *Developing Writer's Assessment (DWA) Grades K–6*, the *Developmental Reading Assessment (DRA2) Grades 4–8*, and the *Developmental Reading Assessment Bridge Kit*.

Introduction

Each year as teachers administer the *Developmental Reading Assessment (DRA2)*, they often discover a number of students who make little or no progress in their ability to read more challenging texts due to inefficient word analysis skills, slow and/or non-fluent reading, insufficient comprehension strategies, or limited understanding of word meanings. To help these at-risk, struggling readers, teachers need to monitor their progress more closely to ensure that each student is benefiting from the instruction he or she is receiving.

The *DRA2 Progress Monitoring Assessment* provides a quick, standardized procedure for teachers to monitor the progress of struggling readers (Tier 2 and Tier 3 students) and to inform instruction. The assessment is administered during a one-on-one conference. Students' oral reading fluency, comprehension, vocabulary, and word reading skills are assessed through the careful analysis of student reading behaviors and oral responses. The assessment can be administered every two to three weeks to confirm effective teaching practices as well as document student progress toward established benchmarks.

The *DRA2 Progress Monitoring Assessment* has been created so that teachers can identify and address specific areas of instruction for struggling readers. Using the assessments to inform instruction will help move students toward grade-level benchmarks. Teachers use multiple, one-page passages at each grade level to monitor incremental changes in student reading behaviors. The assessments can be used to meet state and federal guidelines that require educators to assess reading progress more frequently for students who are reading slightly to significantly below established benchmarks. After establishing

a *DRA2* benchmark level in the beginning of the school year, teachers use the *Progress Monitoring Assessment* passages at students' instructional levels throughout the school year, not only to monitor the progress of their struggling or at-risk readers, but also to identify areas of instructional need for each student. Teachers administer *DRA2* at mid-year and again toward the end of the school year to document progress throughout the year.

Teachers often are in need of immediate teaching strategies and direction on how to follow up with learners after an assessment. The *DRA2 Progress Monitoring Assessment* not only identifies readers' strengths and instructional needs, but also provides suggested instructional interventions for each skill assessed. The *If…then* statements in the Moving into Instruction section, pages 24–118 in this Teacher Guide, provide recommendations for instruction to follow each progress monitoring student passage. For example, **if** a student scores below the independent level for rate, **then** the teacher is directed to have the student practice with repeated readings of the assessment passage to build fluency. The same passage may also be used to reinforce a targeted comprehension skill, such as sequence, by helping the student identify clue words that indicate sequence in the passage. A set of instructional Routine Cards accompanies the *Progress Monitoring Assessment* and offers concrete instructional strategies to be used for teaching word reading, fluency, vocabulary, retelling, and summarizing.

Comparing *DRA2* and the *Progress Monitoring Assessment*

The *Developmental Reading Assessment (DRA2)* and the *DRA2 Progress Monitoring Assessment* have been developed to work in conjunction with one another. Together they provide a comprehensive profile of a reader's strengths and instructional needs. Although both assess oral reading fluency and comprehension, responses on the *Progress Monitoring Assessment* are all oral, not written, in order to provide a progress monitoring tool that can be administered in just a few minutes. In addition, the comprehension strategies and skills in *DRA2* and the *Progress Monitoring Assessment* vary. The *Progress Monitoring Assessment* focuses on retelling fiction passages and identifying main ideas and supporting details in nonfiction passages; it also includes comprehension prompts targeting comparing and contrasting, drawing conclusions, cause-and-effect relationships, and sequence—core skills that will prepare students to respond more effectively to the prompts in *DRA2*.

DRA2	Progress Monitoring Assessment
Purpose	
Identify students' reading strengths and instructional needs	Identify students' reading strengths and instructional needs
Help group students by instructional needs and provide direction for instruction	Help group students by instructional needs and provide direction for instruction
Determine independent or instructional reading levels	Determine instructional needs using instructional level passages
Administer to all students at the beginning and end of the school year to document yearly progress	Administer to struggling readers every two to three weeks to monitor progress and to identify their instructional needs
Features	
One-on-one conference	One-on-one conference
73 benchmark books for Grades K–8	95 one-page passages for Grades 1–6
2 nonfiction benchmark books for Grades 1, 4–8; 4 nonfiction benchmark books for Grades 2–3	7–8 nonfiction passages per grade level
Teacher Observation Guides, including directions and continuums	Teacher Observation Guides, including directions and continuums
Oral comprehension responses (Levels 4–24); written comprehension responses (Levels 28–80)	Oral responses for all prompts (all levels)
Focus for Instruction checklists	*If…then* statements to focus instruction
Oral Reading Fluency	
Monitor accuracy, rate, phrasing, and expression	Monitor accuracy, rate, phrasing, and expression
Comprehension	
Oral retelling (Levels 4–24)	Oral retelling of fiction; analyze character, setting, and plot (all levels)
Written summary and literal comprehension (Levels 28–80)	Oral summary of nonfiction; identify main idea and details (all levels)
Preview, make connections, reflect (Levels 4–16); predict, interpret, reflect (Levels 18–24); written question and predict, interpret, reflect (Levels 28–80); metacognitive awareness (Levels 40–80)	Compare and contrast, cause-and-effect relationships, sequence of events, and draw conclusions (all levels)
Vocabulary used by student (Levels 4–24)	Vocabulary and word reading (all levels)

Developing the *Progress Monitoring Assessment*

The *DRA2 Progress Monitoring Assessment* was developed to give teachers a standardized means to monitor the progress of struggling readers (Tier 2 and Tier 3 students). Grade-level standards were analyzed to determine the fluency, comprehension, and reading skills that it would be necessary to include in an assessment of this type. The Student Passages were written to highlight these skills and to engage the students who would read them. The Student Passages and Teacher Observation Guides were field-tested in 2010–2011 by classroom teachers and reading specialists across the United States. Urban, suburban, rural, and small-town school settings were represented, and the field-testing included representative samples across racial/ethnic, gender, and grade-level groups.

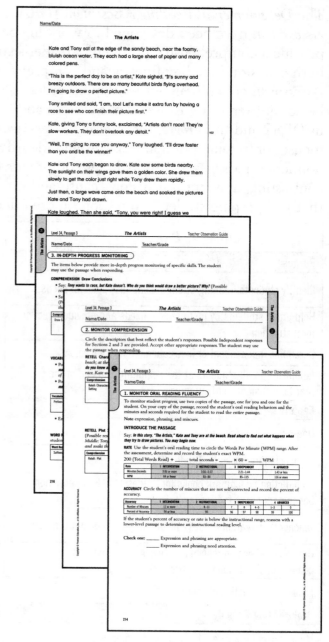

The goals of the *Progress Monitoring Assessment* field-testing were to verify that

- the passages are correctly leveled according to DRA2 levels;

- the skills assessed are developmentally appropriate;

- the assessments are in a developmentally appropriate order;

- the Teacher Observation Guides contain assessment information that is helpful to teachers and will inform instruction;

- the directions and recording forms are clear and manageable.

Student Passages and Teacher Observation Guides were revised based on teacher feedback as well as student performance.

Using Progress Monitoring with English Language Learners

The *Developmental Reading Assessment* as well as *DRA2 Progress Monitoring Assessment* were designed to assess native English speakers. A benefit of using *DRA2* with English language learners (ELLs) is being able to compare their reading levels with those of native English speakers. Teachers should follow the standard procedure and format for assessing all students. However, when assessing ELLs, there are factors that can affect student outcomes. Here are some recommendations:

① **Do not count mispronunciations as reading errors on Records of Oral Reading.** ELLs may have not acquired the ability to form English language sounds, and some may have an accent. During the assessment, mispronunciations should be documented for oral language teaching, but they should not be counted as miscues on the Record of Oral Reading.

② **Use fluency, phrasing, and expression as key indicators of comprehension.** For ELLs, phrasing and expression can be even more helpful than WPM. Some ELLs quickly learn the decoding patterns of English and are able to read fluently, but are unable to comprehend what they read. Phrasing and expression can be the key to denoting comprehension. For the *Progress Monitoring Assessment*, you will be using passages at the student's instructional level. An ELL student may fall into intervention range for rate with a passage because the student is translating while reading. In this case, continue the assessment, but keep in mind that this level would be considered the student's intervention level. To build students' fluency, use lower-level passages so that fluency and comprehension work together.

③ **Use bilingual staff to assess students when possible.** This allows students to give responses to the prompts in their native languages. If many responses are in a student's first language and they are adequate responses, that particular level would be considered his or her instructional level.

④ **Assess in the student's first language.** *Evaluación para verificar el progreso* of *EDL2 (Evaluación del desarrollo de la lectura)* provides teachers of native Spanish speakers a comparable progress monitoring tool.

Implications In teaching ELLs to read and write in English, one must understand that oral language development through literacy is vital. Consider using the following instructional strategies:

- Provide explicit teaching and modeling of language structures, oral language, and reading strategies.

- Arrange opportunities for students to speak English in structured, supportive, and meaningful settings.

- Give students many opportunities to re-read texts.

- Allow students to express themselves in their native language first to help them organize their thoughts before stating them in English.

Olivia Ruiz-Figueroa
EDL2 Author

Each assessment includes a one-page, leveled Student Passage and an accompanying Teacher Observation Guide. This assessment is a brief, one-on-one reading conference that provides in-depth information gained from the analysis of student behaviors and oral responses. The assessment conference includes these parts:

- **Monitor Oral Reading Fluency** The student reads a one-page instructional-level passage in three or fewer minutes as the teacher takes a record of the student's oral reading. The teacher records the student's oral reading rate beginning with Level 14.

- **Monitor Comprehension** Immediately after reading a passage aloud, the student responds orally to teacher prompts that monitor comprehension. For fictional passages, students respond orally to prompts about characters, setting, and plot. For informational passages, students respond orally to prompts about main (important) ideas and supporting details.

- **In-Depth Progress Monitoring** The student then responds to two prompts that assess understanding of the following comprehension skills: compare and contrast, cause and effect, draw conclusions, or sequence of events. To conclude the conference, the student responds to prompts that assess various skills, including multiple-meaning words, use of context clues, and reading words, such as base words and affixes and multisyllabic words.

DRA2 *Progress Monitoring Assessment* Student Passages

The *Progress Monitoring Assessment* can be used to monitor at-risk readers in late first grade through sixth grade. At each grade level the Student Passages are arranged in order of difficulty and include both fiction and nonfiction passages. The printable Student Passages and the Teacher Observation Guides are found on the accompanying CD-ROM in the *Progress Monitoring Assessment* package.

DRA2 Levels	Approximate Grade Level	Number of Progress Monitoring Assessment Passages	Number of Fictional Texts	Number of Nonfiction Texts
4, 6, 8, 10, 12, 14, 16, 18*	1	20	13	7
20, 24, 28	2	15	8	7
30, 34, 38	3	15	7	8
40	4	15	7	8
50	5	15	7	8
60	6	15	7	8

* Level 18 may be included in either first or second grade depending on your school or district.

Name/Date

The Artists

Kate and Tony sat at the edge of the sandy beach, near the foamy, bluish ocean water. They each had a large sheet of paper and many colored pens.

"This is the perfect day to be an artist," Kate sighed. "It's sunny and breezy outdoors. There are so many beautiful birds flying overhead. I'm going to draw a perfect picture."

Tony smiled and said, "I am, too! Let's make it extra fun by having a race to see who can finish their picture first."

Kate, giving Tony a funny look, exclaimed, "Artists don't race! They're slow workers. They don't overlook any detail."

102

Name/Date

Mike and Pete

Mike has a big dog. His name is Pete.
Pete can run very fast.
Mike and Pete like to race.
Mike and Pete race to the lake.

They run up a hill.
They run around a little tree.
They run down a hill.
They run around a big tree.

Then they come to the lake.
Did Mike win? Did Pete win?
It is a tie!

Mike and Pete both came in first!
Nice race, Mike! Nice race, Pete!

78

Level 8, Passage 2

Level 34, Student Passage 3
Level 8, Student Passage 2

The *DRA2 Progress Monitoring Assessment* passages, Levels 4–60, were carefully developed, field-tested, and revised to ensure that they are grade-level appropriate, arranged in order of difficulty, and appealing to elementary-age students. The following elements were also incorporated:

- concepts and experiences common to a majority of elementary-age students
- repetitive language at Levels 4–10
- one picture per passage at Levels 4–18
- accessible vocabulary and word choice
- appropriate sentence length and complexity for each level
- passage length suitable for reading in three or fewer minutes

Introduction

Preparing for the Assessment

STEP 1 Prepare a list of students who are reading below grade level according to *DRA2* benchmarks. Check to see that you have the necessary Student Passages and accompanying Teacher Observation Guides for the assessment conferences you will be conducting. Select a *Progress Monitoring Assessment* passage that is on the student's Instructional level. To find an Instructional level, go up one level from the student's most recent DRA2 Independent level.

STEP 2 Assemble assessment materials. For each student being assessed, you will need:
- one copy of the appropriate Teacher Observation Guide
- two copies of the Student Passage—one for the student to read and one for you to record observations on

You will also need:
- a timer to time each student's reading
- a calculator to determine each student's exact number of words per minute, or wpm
- a pen or pencil to use for recording
- a stapler to staple the record of oral reading and Teacher Observation Guide together after the assessment
- a quiet space with a table and two chairs so you and your student can focus on the assessment

STEP 3 Review, if needed, how to take and analyze a record of oral reading. Directions for taking a record of oral reading appear on page 13.

STEP 4 Preview the Teacher Observation Guide for each passage you intend to use.

A record of oral reading is an assessment of a student's oral reading accuracy, rate, phrasing, and expression. Reading accuracy is based on the number of words read correctly. Reading rate is based on the number of words read per minute.

The Artists

① *W*
Kate and <u>Tony</u> sat at the edge of the
② *R*
sandy beach, near the foamy, bluish
ocean water. They each had a large
③   ④ *sc*
sheet of paper and many colored
pens.

⑤ *T*
"This is the <u>perfect</u> day to be an
⑥ *very*
artist," Kate sighed. "It's sunny and
breezy outdoors. There are so many
beautiful birds flying overhead. I'm
going to draw a perfect picture."

Tony smiled and said, "I am, too!
Let's make it extra fun by having
⑦
a race to see who can finish their
picture first."

Kate, giving Tony a funny look,
exclaimed, "Artists don't race!
They're slow workers. They don't
⑧   ⑨ */de/tells/*
overlook (any) detail."

"Well, I'm going to race you anyway,"
Tony laughed. "I'll draw faster than
you and be the winner!"

Level 34, Passage 3

Include the following on the Record of Oral Reading, but do not count as miscues:

① **Long Pauses** The student pauses at a word. Pauses are not counted as errors but impact fluency.

② **Repetition** The student repeats a word or words. Repetitions are not counted as errors but impact fluency.

③ **Sounding Out** The student correctly sounds out a word. This is not counted as an error.

④ **Self-correction** The student reads a word incorrectly but then corrects the error. Self-corrections are not counted as errors. However, noting self-corrections will help you identify words the student finds difficult.

On the record of Oral Reading, count each miscue as one error:

⑤ **Word Told by Teacher** Teacher provides word to student when student is unable to decode it.

⑥ **Insertion** The student inserts a word or parts of words that are not in the text.

⑦ **Reversal** The student reverses the order of two words.

⑧ **Omission** The student omits words or word parts.

⑨ **Substitution** The student substitutes words or parts of words for the words in the text, mispronounces a word, or sounds out a word incorrectly.

Conducting the Assessment Conference

STEP 1   MONITOR ORAL READING FLUENCY

- Follow the directions on the Teacher Observation Guide. Please note that what you are to say to the student (the prompt) is in bold type.

- Give the student a copy of the Student Passage to be read aloud.

- Introduce the passage.

- Take a record of oral reading. Begin timing the passage when the student begins reading the passage and not before. (For Levels 4 through 12, only accuracy is marked on the Teacher Observation Guide.)

- Time the student's oral reading to determine his or her reading rate for students reading at Level 14 and above. Record the student's reading time on the line at the bottom of your copy of the passage.

- Circle the student's reading time and the wpm on the continuum.

- Count the number of miscues not self-corrected. Then circle the number of miscues and the percent of accuracy on the continuum.

Note If the student's percent of accuracy or wpm fall below the Instructional range on the continuum, stop the assessment. Plan to reassess at another time with a lower-level passage to find the student's Instructional level.

If the student's percent of accuracy and wpm fall in the Independent range, complete the assessment to determine if any instructional needs are identified.

The Artists

34

| Level 34, Passage 3 | *The Artists* | Teacher Observation Guide |

Name/Date _____ Teacher/Grade _____

1. MONITOR ORAL READING FLUENCY

❶ To monitor student progress, use two copies of the passage, one for you and one for the student. On your copy of the passage, record the student's oral reading behaviors and the minutes and seconds required for the student to read the entire passage.

Note expression, phrasing, and miscues.

INTRODUCE THE PASSAGE

❷ Say: *In this story, "The Artists," Kate and Tony are at the beach. Read aloud to find out what happens when they try to draw pictures. You may begin now.*

❸ **RATE** Use the student's oral reading time to circle the Words Per Minute (WPM) range. After the assessment, determine and record the student's exact WPM.

200 (Total Words Read) ÷ _____ total seconds = _____ × 60 = _____ WPM

❹

Rate	1 INTERVENTION	2 INSTRUCTIONAL	3 INDEPENDENT	4 ADVANCED
Minutes:Seconds	3:06 or more	3:05–2:22	2:21–1:44	1:43 or less
WPM	64 or fewer	65–84	85–115	116 or more

ACCURACY Circle the number of miscues that are not self-corrected and record the percent of accuracy.

❺

Accuracy	1 INTERVENTION	2 INSTRUCTIONAL	3 INDEPENDENT			4 ADVANCED	
Number of Miscues	12 or more	8–11	7	6	4–5	1–3	0
Percent of Accuracy	94 or less	95	96	97	98	99	100

If the student's percent of accuracy or rate is below the instructional range, reassess with a lower-level passage to determine an instructional reading level.

Check one: _____ Expression and phrasing are appropriate.

_____ Expression and phrasing need attention.

214

Teacher Observation Guide

Each Teacher Observation Guide includes teacher directions, questions, and prompts for the corresponding student assessment passage. There are four parts to each assessment: **1.** Monitor Oral Reading Fluency; **2.** Monitor Comprehension; **3.** In-Depth Progress Monitoring; **4.** Focus and Analysis for Instruction.

❶ Directions are provided for setting up and administering the assessment: criteria for evaluation and scoring guidelines are also included.

❷ Bold, italicized text indicates what the teacher is to say to the student to effectively guide him or her through the assessment.

❸ A simple equation is provided to determine the student's exact words-per-minute rate.

❹ A scoring continuum follows each set of prompts. The continuums reflect four types of responses: Intervention (Emerging for lower levels), Instructional (Developing for lower levels), Independent, and Advanced.

❺ All miscues not self-corrected are counted, and the number is circled in the chart to determine the student's percentage of accuracy.

Assessment Guidelines

Students may use the passage to respond to prompts in Steps 2 and 3. To ensure that this assessment is standardized, it is important not to give the student additional information or prompts or to ask other questions. It is acceptable to substitute terms familiar to the student if those in the assessment are not generally used in your classroom; for example, using *order of events* instead of *sequence of events*.

STEP 2   MONITOR COMPREHENSION

- Read aloud the questions and prompts provided.

- Record notes of the student's responses on the Teacher Observation Guide.

STEP 3   IN-DEPTH PROGRESS MONITORING

- Read aloud the questions and prompts provided to monitor the student's control of specific reading skills or strategies.

- Record notes of the student's responses on the Teacher Observation Guide.

- End the assessment conference by thanking the student and commenting on what he or she did well.

Note When one or more of the descriptors in Step 1 or Step 2 fall in the Instructional or Intervention range, the passage can be considered Instructional.

If the student's Oral Reading Fluency (Step 1) and Comprehension (Step 2) descriptors fall in the Independent or Advanced range, use a higher-level passage in order to determine the student's Instructional level.

Level 34, Passage 3   **The Artists**   Teacher Observation Guide

Name/Date _____ Teacher/Grade _____

(2. MONITOR COMPREHENSION)

Circle the descriptors that best reflect the student's responses. Possible Independent responses for Sections 2 and 3 are provided. Accept other appropriate responses. The student may use the passage when responding.

RETELL Character/Setting Say: *What is the setting of the story?* (Possible responses: *at the edge of a beach; at the ocean*) *Who are the characters are in the story?* (Possible response: *Kate and Tony*) *What do you know about these characters?* (Possible responses: *They are drawing pictures. Tony wants to race. Kate wants to work slowly, like an artist.*)

Comprehension	1 INTERVENTION	2 INSTRUCTIONAL	3 INDEPENDENT	4 ADVANCED
Retell: Character/ Setting	Does not identify characters or setting, or does not respond	Gives a partially correct response, such as identifies 1 character and the setting; may misinterpret information	Identifies setting and characters and provides 1 detail about each character	Identifies setting and characters; provides details about each character using specific vocabulary from the story

RETELL Plot Say: *Tell me what happens at the beginning, in the middle, and at the end of the story.*
(Possible responses: *Beginning: Kate and Tony are at the beach. They are going to draw pictures. Middle: Tony wants to have a race to see who can finish first. End: A wave comes onto the beach and soaks their pictures. Kate says they should have raced the waves.*)

Comprehension	1 INTERVENTION	2 INSTRUCTIONAL	3 INDEPENDENT	4 ADVANCED
Retell: Plot	Identifies none of the plot's events or does not respond	Gives a partially correct response, such as identifies 1–2 plot events; may misinterpret events	Identifies plot events from the beginning, middle, and end of the story	Identifies plot events from the beginning, middle, and end of the story including details and specific vocabulary

Level 34, Passage 3   **The Artists**   Teacher Observation Guide

Name/Date _____ Teacher/Grade _____

(3. IN-DEPTH PROGRESS MONITORING)

The items below provide more in-depth progress monitoring of specific skills. The student may use the passage when responding.

COMPREHENSION Draw Conclusions
- Say: *Tony wants to race, but Kate doesn't. Who do you think would draw a better picture? Why?* (Possible response: *Kate would draw a better picture because she would take her time.*)
- Say: *Where do you think Kate and Tony will sit the next time they decide to draw pictures at the beach?* (Possible response: *They will sit farther away from the ocean's edge so the waves don't ruin their pictures.*)

Comprehension	1 INTERVENTION	2 INSTRUCTIONAL	3 INDEPENDENT	4 ADVANCED
Draw Conclusions	Does not draw a conclusion or does not respond	Gives a partially correct response, such as draws 1 of 2 conclusions	Draws a reasonable conclusion using information from the text for each question	Draws a perceptive conclusion using information and specific vocabulary from the story for each question

VOCABULARY Suffixes
- Point to the word *artist* in the second paragraph. Say: *This word is* **artist**. *What does this word mean?* (Possible responses: *person who creates drawings, paintings, sculptures, or other works of art*)
- Point to the word *bluish* in the first paragraph. Say: *This word is* **bluish**. *What does this word mean?* (Possible responses: bluish *means "somewhat blue in color"*)

Vocabulary	1 INTERVENTION	2 INSTRUCTIONAL	3 INDEPENDENT	4 ADVANCED
Prefixes and Suffixes	Gives inaccurate or vague meanings, or does not respond	Gives a partially correct response, such as the intended meaning of 1 word	Gives the intended meaning of each word	Gives the intended meaning with details for each word

- End conference.

WORD READING Suffixes Return to the Record of Oral Reading to determine whether the student read these words correctly: *sandy, bluish, workers, golden.*

Word Reading	1 INTERVENTION	2 INSTRUCTIONAL	3 INDEPENDENT	4 ADVANCED
Suffixes	Does not read any words accurately or omits them	Reads 1–3 of 4 words accurately	Reads all 4 words accurately	Reads all 4 words accurately and automatically

Teacher Observation Guide

❻ All *DRA2* progress monitoring passages assess a student's ability either to summarize important facts and details in nonfiction text or to retell characters, setting, and plot in fictional text.

❼ In-Depth Progress Monitoring provides additional assessment opportunities for comprehension, vocabulary, and word-reading skills.

Assessment Guidelines

Analyzing Student Responses and Selecting a Focus for Instruction

STEP 1 Analyze student responses and circle or highlight the appropriate performance level on the continuums in the Teacher Observation Guides. Possible responses have been provided for each question about the passages. However, students may provide other correct responses using their own words.

- Select an **Intervention**-level descriptor on the continuum when students give an incorrect response or they do not give a response.

- Select an **Instructional**-level descriptor on the continuum when students give a partially correct response.

- Select an **Independent**-level descriptor when students give a correct response.

- Select an **Advanced**-level descriptor when students include details and vocabulary from the text and/or give thoughtful, insightful responses.

STEP 2 Record assessment results on the printable *Progress Monitoring Assessment* Fluency Progress Chart and the Student Progress Monitoring Record found on the CD-ROM.

STEP 3 Select one or two areas in which the student scored below the Independent range as the focus for instruction.

STEP 4 If you wish, record the student's continuum scores on the printable *Progress Monitoring Assessment* Group Recording Form found on the CD-ROM and use the information to group students for instruction based on common needs.

Fluency Progress Charts

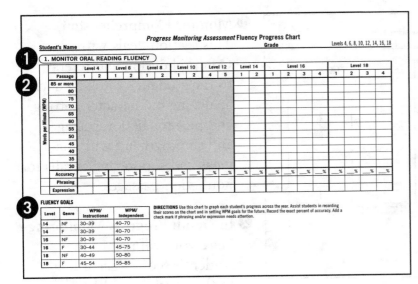

Fluency Progress Chart

❶ Oral Reading Fluency On the *DRA2 Progress Monitoring Assessment* CD-ROM, you will find Fluency Progress Charts for Levels 4–18, Levels 18–28, Levels 30–38, Level 40, Level 50, and Level 60.

❷ Graph Use these printable charts to graph students' progress throughout the year. Assist students in recording their own scores on the chart and setting wpm goals for the future. Record wpm for rate and record a percentage for accuracy. Check expression and/or phrasing if those areas need attention.

❸ Fluency Goals Fluency goals for fiction and nonfiction at each level are identified on each fluency chart.

Student and Group Recording Forms

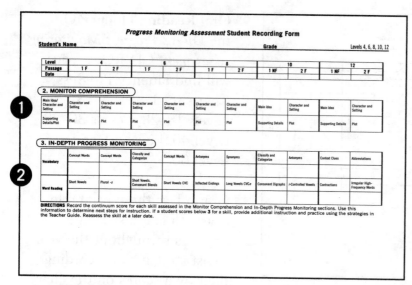

Student Recording Form

Group Recording Form

❶ Monitor Comprehension
This section deals with Comprehension and refers to the student's retelling and analyzing of character, setting, and plot for fiction passages, and summarizing with main ideas and supporting details for nonfiction passages.

❷ In-Depth Progress Monitoring
Here you will record the student's scores (according to the continuums) for the comprehension strategy or skill, the vocabulary skill, and the word-reading skill that were assessed with a particular passage.

❸ Group Recording Form
This printable form, also found on the CD-ROM, can help you identify which students to group for instruction.

Using Moving into Instruction

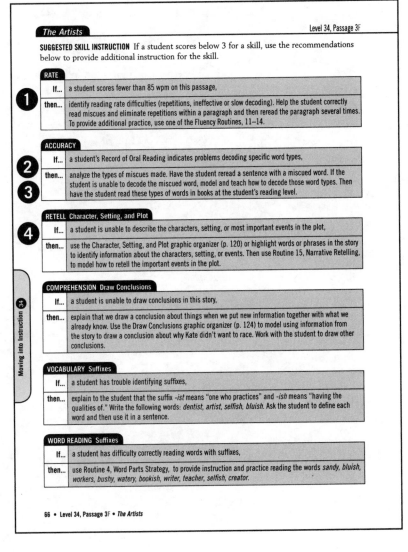

The Artists   Level 34, Passage 3F

SUGGESTED SKILL INSTRUCTION If a student scores below 3 for a skill, use the recommendations below to provide additional instruction for the skill.

RATE

If... a student scores fewer than 85 wpm on this passage,

then... identify reading rate difficulties (repetitions, ineffective or slow decoding). Help the student correctly read miscues and eliminate repetitions within a paragraph and then reread the paragraph several times. To provide additional practice, use one of the Fluency Routines, 11–14.

ACCURACY

If... a student's Record of Oral Reading indicates problems decoding specific word types,

then... analyze the types of miscues made. Have the student reread a sentence with a miscued word. If the student is unable to decode the miscued word, model and teach how to decode those word types. Then have the student read these types of words in books at the student's reading level.

RETELL Character, Setting, and Plot

If... a student is unable to describe the characters, setting, or most important events in the plot,

then... use the Character, Setting, and Plot graphic organizer (p. 120) or highlight words or phrases in the story to identify information about the characters, setting, or events. Then use Routine 15, Narrative Retelling, to model how to retell the important events in the plot.

COMPREHENSION Draw Conclusions

If... a student is unable to draw conclusions in this story,

then... explain that we draw a conclusion about things when we put new information together with what we already know. Use the Draw Conclusions graphic organizer (p. 124) to model using information from the story to draw a conclusion about why Kate didn't want to race. Work with the student to draw other conclusions.

VOCABULARY Suffixes

If... a student has trouble identifying suffixes,

then... explain to the student that the suffix *-ist* means "one who practices" and *-ish* means "having the qualities of." Write the following words: *dentist, artist, selfish, bluish*. Ask the student to define each word and then use it in a sentence.

WORD READING Suffixes

If... a student has difficulty correctly reading words with suffixes,

then... use Routine 4, Word Parts Strategy, to provide instruction and practice reading the words *sandy, bluish, workers, bushy, watery, bookish, writer, teacher, selfish, creator.*

Moving into Instruction 34

66 • Level 34, Passage 3F • *The Artists*

Moving into Instruction begins on page 23 of this Teacher Guide. These pages provide recommendations for instruction to follow each progress monitoring assessment.

1 *If...then* statements are included for each Student Passage.

2 Recommendations for instructional follow-up are provided for every skill assessed with a Student Passage.

3 Use the *If...then* statements for instructional direction for any skill in which a student scores below the Independent range on the continuums.

4 Instructional Routine Cards and reproducible graphic organizers can be used for follow-up instruction. Some Routine Cards reference Sound-Spelling Cards, which also appear on the CD-ROM. The graphic organizers can be found both in this Teacher Guide, pp. 119–125, and on the CD-ROM.

Assessment Guidelines

Moving into Instruction

Use these recommendations for instruction following each progress monitoring assessment. Additional resources referenced in the *If…then* statements include the Routine Cards, which are part of the *DRA2 Progress Monitoring Assessment* kit, and graphic organizers, which can be found both on the CD-ROM and in this Teacher Guide, pp. 119–125.

SUGGESTED SKILL INSTRUCTION If a student scores below 3 for a skill, use the recommendations below to provide additional instruction for the skill.

ACCURACY

If...	a student's Record of Oral Reading indicates problems decoding specific word types,
then...	analyze the types of miscues made. Have the student reread a sentence with a miscued word. If the student is unable to decode the miscued word, model and teach how to decode those word types. Then have the student read these types of words in books at the student's reading level.

RETELL Plot

If...	a student is unable to retell the plot of the story,
then...	reread the first four lines of the story and use the Plot section of the Character, Setting, and Plot graphic organizer (p. 120) to identify the first thing Pig does in the mud. The student may draw pictures or use words. Then help the student determine the other two things Pig does as the student rereads lines 5–8.

VOCABULARY Concept Words

If...	a student has trouble identifying the meanings of concept words,
then...	point to each concept word the student was unable to identify and read the word aloud. Provide a simple, student-friendly definition and use the word in a context sentence. Then have the student use the same word in his or her own sentence. Repeat with other concept words, such as *rolled*.

WORD READING Short Vowels

If...	a student has difficulty correctly reading words with short vowels,
then...	use Routine 1, Sound-by-Sound Blending, to provide instruction and practice reading the words *mud, fun, yes, Pig, ran, sat, cab, dad, big, mom, hop, bed, wet, bus, cup*.

Moving into Instruction 4

SUGGESTED SKILL INSTRUCTION If a student scores below 3 for a skill, use the recommendations below to provide additional instruction for the skill.

ACCURACY

If...	a student's Record of Oral Reading indicates problems decoding specific word types,
then...	analyze the types of miscues made. Have the student reread a sentence with a miscued word. If the student is unable to decode the miscued word, model and teach how to decode those word types. Then have the student read these types of words in books at the student's reading level.

RETELL Character and Plot

If...	a student is unable to retell details about the characters or the most important events of the story,
then...	use the Character, Setting, and Plot graphic organizer (p. 120) or highlight words and phrases in the story to identify the characters or events. Have the student reread the first part of the story and tell what happens first. Then help him or her determine what happens next and last while rereading the rest of the story.

VOCABULARY Concept Words

If...	a student has trouble identifying the meanings of concept words,
then...	point to each concept word the student was unable to identify and read the word aloud. Provide a simple, student-friendly definition and use the word in a context sentence. Then have the student use the same word in his or her own sentence. Repeat with other concept words, such as *sun* and *run*.

WORD READING Plural *-s*

If...	a student has difficulty correctly reading words with the plural ending *-s,*
then...	use Routine 1, Sound-by-Sound Blending, to provide instruction and practice reading the words *dogs, cats, pets, bags, rats, kids, hogs, hens, pigs, bugs, hugs.*

Moving into Instruction ④

SUGGESTED SKILL INSTRUCTION If a student scores below 3 for a skill, use the recommendations below to provide additional instruction for the skill.

ACCURACY

If...	a student's Record of Oral Reading indicates problems decoding specific word types,
then...	analyze the types of miscues made. Have the student reread a sentence with a miscued word. If the student is unable to decode the miscued word, model and teach how to decode those word types. Then have the student read these types of words in books at the student's reading level.

RETELL Character and Plot

If...	a student is unable to describe the characters or retell the events of the story,
then...	read the first sentence of the story and model how to identify a character by highlighting the proper noun that names the character. Then have the student reread the first part of the story and tell what happens first. Help the student determine what happens next and last while rereading the rest of the story together.

VOCABULARY Classify/Categorize

If...	a student has trouble categorizing words,
then...	use the T-Chart graphic organizer (p. 125) to model how you would group the animals in the story into a group called *pets,* as you reread the first three lines and think aloud. Then work with the student to categorize color words from the passage using the same method. Together add other known examples to each category.

WORD READING Short Vowels; Consonant Blends; Final *-ck, -ll*

If...	a student has difficulty correctly reading words with short vowels, consonant blends, or final *-ck, -ll,*
then...	use Routine 2, Whole-Word Blending, to provide instruction and practice reading the words *Pam, pets, Bill, duck, swim, fast, back, Jill, luck, clap, drip, hill, pick, list.*

SUGGESTED SKILL INSTRUCTION If a student scores below 3 for a skill, use the recommendations below to provide additional instruction for the skill.

ACCURACY

If...	a student's Record of Oral Reading indicates problems decoding specific word types,
then...	analyze the types of miscues made. Have the student reread a sentence with a miscued word. If the student is unable to decode the miscued word, model and teach how to decode those word types. Then have the student read these types of words in books at the student's reading level.

RETELL Character and Plot

If...	a student is unable to describe the characters or most important events from the story,
then...	use the Character, Setting, and Plot graphic organizer (p. 120) or highlight words and phrases in the story to identify information about the characters or events. Then use Routine 15, Narrative Retelling, to model how to retell the important events in the plot.

VOCABULARY Concept Words

If...	a student has trouble identifying the meanings of concept words,
then...	point to each concept word the student was unable to identify and read the word aloud. Provide a simple, student-friendly definition and use the word in a context sentence. Then have the student use the same word in his or her own sentence. Repeat with other concept words, such as *baby* or *mother*.

WORD READING Short Vowels CVC

If...	a student has difficulty correctly reading words with short vowels,
then...	use Routine 1, Sound-by-Sound Blending, to provide instruction and practice reading the words *hen, cat, pig, did, not, bed, fin, top, fan, sad, pop, pin, run, pup, hat, ten.*

Moving into Instruction 6

SUGGESTED SKILL INSTRUCTION If a student scores below 3 for a skill, use the recommendations below to provide additional instruction for the skill.

ACCURACY

If...	a student's Record of Oral Reading indicates problems decoding specific word types,
then...	analyze the types of miscues made. Have the student reread a sentence with a miscued word. If the student is unable to decode the miscued word, model and teach how to decode those word types. Then have the student read these types of words in books at the student's reading level.

RETELL Character, Setting, and Plot

If...	a student is unable to describe the characters, setting, or most important events in the plot,
then...	use the Character, Setting, and Plot graphic organizer (p. 120) or highlight words or phrases in the story to identify information about the characters, setting, or events. Then use Routine 15, Narrative Retelling, to model how to retell the important events in the plot.

VOCABULARY Antonyms

If...	a student has trouble identifying the meanings of antonyms,
then...	write a list of familiar adjectives such as *little, new,* and *happy*. Help the student read each word and tell you what the word means. Then work with him or her to identify a word with the opposite meaning.

WORD READING Inflected Endings

If...	a student has difficulty correctly reading words with inflected endings,
then...	use Routine 4, Word Parts Strategy, to provide instruction and practice reading the words *missed, picks, feeling, sees, smiles, jumps, missing, mixed, seeing, takes, falling*.

Moving into Instruction ⑧

SUGGESTED SKILL INSTRUCTION If a student scores below 3 for a skill, use the recommendations below to provide additional instruction for the skill.

ACCURACY

If...	a student's Record of Oral Reading indicates problems decoding specific word types,
then...	analyze the types of miscues made. Have the student reread a sentence with a miscued word. If the student is unable to decode the miscued word, model and teach how to decode those word types. Then have the student read these types of words in books at the student's reading level.

RETELL Character, Setting, and Plot

If...	a student is unable to describe the characters, setting, or most important events in the plot,
then...	use the Character, Setting, and Plot graphic organizer (p. 120) or highlight words or phrases in the story to identify information about the characters, setting, or events. Then use Routine 15, Narrative Retelling, to model how to retell the important events in the plot.

VOCABULARY Synonyms

If...	a student has trouble identifying synonyms,
then...	use the T-Chart graphic organizer (p. 125) and write *big, fast,* and *little* in the left column. Ask the student to read each word and tell you what it means. Then work with him or her to identify another word that has the same meaning. Write the synonyms in the right column of the chart.

WORD READING Long Vowels CVC*e*

If...	a student has difficulty correctly reading words with long vowels,
then...	use Routine 3, Vowel-First Blending, to provide instruction and practice reading the words *name, like, race, lake, came, nice, cane, pine, make, rose, cape, made, time.*

Moving into Instruction ❽

SUGGESTED SKILL INSTRUCTION If a student scores below 3 for a skill, use the recommendations below to provide additional instruction for the skill.

ACCURACY

If...	a student's Record of Oral Reading indicates problems decoding specific word types,
then...	analyze the types of miscues made. Have the student reread a sentence with a miscued word. If the student is unable to decode the miscued word, model and teach how to decode those word types. Then have the student read these types of words in books at the student's reading level.

SUMMARIZE

If...	a student is unable to identify important ideas or details in this passage,
then...	model how to identify an important idea and the details that support it as you read aloud part of the passage. Then have the student do the same with the remainder of the passage. Use Routine 16, Summarizing, for additional instruction and practice.

VOCABULARY Classify/Categorize

If...	a student has trouble sorting words into categories,
then...	use the T-Chart graphic organizer (p. 125) and model how to identify living things to record on one side of the chart. Then work with the student to identify and record things that are not living on the other side of the chart. Together add other examples to each category.

WORD READING Consonant Digraphs *sh, th, wh*

If...	a student has difficulty correctly reading words with these consonant digraphs,
then...	use Routine 1, Sound-by-Sound Blending, to provide instruction and practice reading the words *what, this, that, shed, these, things, ship, math, wash, whale, wheel, three.*

SUGGESTED SKILL INSTRUCTION If a student scores below 3 for a skill, use the recommendations below to provide additional instruction for the skill.

ACCURACY

If...	a student's Record of Oral Reading indicates problems decoding specific word types,
then...	analyze the types of miscues made. Have the student reread a sentence with a miscued word. If the student is unable to decode the miscued word, model and teach how to decode those word types. Then have the student read these types of words in books at the student's reading level.

RETELL Character, Setting, and Plot

If...	a student is unable to describe the characters, setting, or most important events in the plot,
then...	use the Character, Setting, and Plot graphic organizer (p. 120) or highlight words or phrases in the story to identify information about the characters, setting, or events. Then use Routine 15, Narrative Retelling, to model how to retell the important events in the plot.

VOCABULARY Antonyms

If...	a student has trouble identifying the meanings of antonyms,
then...	write a list of familiar words, such as *down, warm, small*, and *find*. Ask the student to read each word and tell you what it means. Then work with him or her to identify a word with the opposite meaning.

WORD READING *r*-Controlled Vowels

If...	a student has difficulty correctly reading words with *r*-controlled vowels,
then...	use Routine 1, Sound-by-Sound Blending, to provide instruction and practice reading the words *Mark, yard, March, bird, tar, sir, fur, her, for, third, car, jar.*

Moving into Instruction 10

SUGGESTED SKILL INSTRUCTION If a student scores below 3 for a skill, use the recommendations below to provide additional instruction for the skill.

ACCURACY

If...	a student's Record of Oral Reading indicates problems decoding specific word types,
then...	analyze the types of miscues made. Have the student reread a sentence with a miscued word. If the student is unable to decode the miscued word, model and teach how to decode those word types. Then have the student read these types of words in books at the student's reading level.

SUMMARIZE

If...	a student is unable to identify important ideas or details in this passage,
then...	model how to identify an important idea and the details that support it as you read aloud part of the passage. Then have the student do the same with the remainder of the passage. Use Routine 16, Summarizing, for additional instruction and practice.

VOCABULARY Context Clues

If...	a student has trouble identifying and using context clues to determine the meanings of words,
then...	read the first four sentences of the passage and think aloud to show how you find words and phrases near the word *spend* that provide clues to its meaning. Then have the student read the second paragraph and work with you to figure out the meaning of the word *save*.

WORD READING Contractions

If...	a student has difficulty correctly reading words with contractions,
then...	use Routine 1, Sound-by-Sound Blending, to provide instruction and practice reading the words *I'm, won't, it's, I'll, isn't, can't, didn't*.

SUGGESTED SKILL INSTRUCTION If a student scores below 3 for a skill, use the recommendations below to provide additional instruction for the skill.

ACCURACY

If...	a student's Record of Oral Reading indicates problems decoding specific word types,
then...	analyze the types of miscues made. Have the student reread a sentence with a miscued word. If the student is unable to decode the miscued word, model and teach how to decode those word types. Then have the student read these types of words in books at the student's reading level.

RETELL Character, Setting, and Plot

If...	a student is unable to describe the characters, setting, or most important events in the plot,
then...	use the Character, Setting, and Plot graphic organizer (p. 120) or highlight words or phrases in the story to identify information about the characters, setting, or events. Then use Routine 15, Narrative Retelling, to model how to retell the important events in the plot.

VOCABULARY Abbreviations

If...	a student has trouble identifying abbreviations,
then...	highlight the abbreviations in the story and use the T-Chart graphic organizer (p. 125) to list these abbreviations in the right column and the words for which they stand in the left column. Together with the student, add other abbreviations *(Mr., St., Rd.)* and help the student read each one and use it in a sentence.

WORD READING Irregular High-Frequency Words

If...	a student has difficulty correctly reading irregular high-frequency words,
then...	use Routine 8, Nondecodable Words Strategy, to provide instruction and practice reading the words *was, we, eat, said, you, she, the, come, they, some, want, be.*

Moving into Instruction 12

SUGGESTED SKILL INSTRUCTION If a student scores below 3 for a skill, use the recommendations below to provide additional instruction for the skill.

RATE

If...	a student scores fewer than 40 wpm on this passage,
then...	identify reading rate difficulties (repetitions, ineffective or slow decoding). Help the student correctly read miscues and eliminate repetitions within a paragraph and then reread the paragraph several times. To provide additional practice, use one of the Fluency Routines, 11–14.

ACCURACY

If...	a student's Record of Oral Reading indicates problems decoding specific word types,
then...	analyze the types of miscues made. Have the student reread a sentence with a miscued word. If the student is unable to decode the miscued word, model and teach how to decode those word types. Then have the student read these types of words in books at the student's reading level.

SUMMARIZE

If...	a student is unable to identify important ideas or details in this passage,
then...	model how to identify an important idea and the details that support it as you read aloud part of the passage. Then have the student do the same with the remainder of the passage. Use Routine 16, Summarizing, for additional instruction and practice.

COMPREHENSION Draw Conclusions

If...	a student is unable to draw conclusions from this passage,
then...	explain that we draw a conclusion about things when we put new information together with what we already know. Reread the passage. Think aloud using information in the passage to draw a conclusion about the reason some plants might die. Then work with the student to draw other conclusions.

VOCABULARY Multiple-Meaning Words

If...	a student cannot identify the correct meanings for the multiple-meanings words in the selection,
then...	model using different definitions of the word *bright* (reflecting light; having a vivid color; intelligent) in context and discuss which one makes the most sense in this passage. Help the student use this method to determine the correct meaning of the word *yard* or *watch*.

WORD READING Long Vowel Digraphs *ai, ay, ee*

If...	a student has difficulty correctly reading words with these long vowel digraphs,
then...	use Routine 2, Whole-Word Blending, to provide instruction and practice reading the words *need, daytime, rain, may, tail, pain, bee, feet, sail, seed, pay, say.*

Moving into Instruction 14

SUGGESTED SKILL INSTRUCTION If a student scores below 3 for a skill, use the recommendations below to provide additional instruction for the skill.

RATE

If...	a student scores fewer than 40 wpm on this passage,
then...	identify reading rate difficulties (repetitions, ineffective or slow decoding). Help the student correctly read miscues and eliminate repetitions within a paragraph and then reread the paragraph several times. To provide additional practice, use one of the Fluency Routines, 11–14.

ACCURACY

If...	a student's Record of Oral Reading indicates problems decoding specific word types,
then...	analyze the types of miscues made. Have the student reread a sentence with a miscued word. If the student is unable to decode the miscued word, model and teach how to decode those word types. Then have the student read these types of words in books at the student's reading level.

RETELL Character, Setting, and Plot

If...	a student is unable to describe the characters, setting, or most important events in the plot,
then...	use the Character, Setting, and Plot graphic organizer (p. 120) or highlight words or phrases in the story to identify information about the characters, setting, or events. Then use Routine 15, Narrative Retelling, to model how to retell the important events in the plot.

COMPREHENSION Sequence

If...	a student is unable to identify sequence in this selection,
then...	begin to read aloud the passage and model how to identify (circle or highlight) the first clue word that signals sequence or time order *(first)*. Have the student read aloud the rest of the passage and help him or her identify other clue words *(then, again)* in the same manner.

VOCABULARY Synonyms

If...	a student has trouble identifying synonyms,
then...	use the T-Chart graphic organizer (p. 125) and write *fast* and *finish* in the left column. Ask the student to read each word and tell what it means, and then say another word that has the same meaning. Write the synonyms in the right column of the chart. Add other words such as *began* and *race*.

WORD READING Inflected Endings

If...	a student has difficulty correctly reading words with inflected endings,
then...	use Routine 4, Word Parts Strategy, to provide instruction and practice reading the words *getting, tied, tripped, branches, stopped, saved, running, crunches, stopped, hopping, brushes*.

Moving into Instruction 14

SUGGESTED SKILL INSTRUCTION If a student scores below 3 for a skill, use the recommendations below to provide additional instruction for the skill.

RATE

If...	a student scores fewer than 45 wpm on this passage,
then...	identify reading rate difficulties (repetitions, ineffective or slow decoding). Help the student correctly read miscues and eliminate repetitions within a paragraph and then reread the paragraph several times. To provide additional practice, use one of the Fluency Routines, 11–14.

ACCURACY

If...	a student's Record of Oral Reading indicates problems decoding specific word types,
then...	analyze the types of miscues made. Have the student reread a sentence with a miscued word. If the student is unable to decode the miscued word, model and teach how to decode those word types. Then have the student read these types of words in books at the student's reading level.

RETELL Character, Setting, and Plot

If...	a student is unable to describe the characters, setting, or most important events in the plot,
then...	use the Character, Setting, and Plot graphic organizer (p. 120) or highlight words or phrases in the story to identify information about the characters, setting, or events. Then use Routine 15, Narrative Retelling, model how to retell the important events in the plot.

COMPREHENSION Cause and Effect

If...	a student is unable to identify cause and effect in the text,
then...	explain certain things cause other things to happen; e.g., you wear a coat (effect) because it's cold outside (cause). Then, using the Cause and Effect graphic organizer (p. 123), model how to find out and record why Todd was sometimes sad. Together with the student, record what Todd did after he grew legs.

VOCABULARY Antonyms

If...	a student has trouble identifying the meanings of antonyms,
then...	use the T-Chart graphic organizer (p. 125) and write *fast* and *happy* in the left column. Ask the student to read each word, tell you what it means, and then say a word that has the opposite meaning. Write the antonyms in the right column of the chart. Repeat with other words: *older, sad, lost*.

WORD READING Short Vowels and Long Vowel Digraphs

If...	a student has difficulty correctly reading words with short vowels and long vowel digraphs,
then...	use Routine 3, Vowel-First Blending, to provide instruction and practice reading the words *Todd, Toad, bet, beat, ran, rain, pan, pain, net, neat, pal, pail, rod, road*.

SUGGESTED SKILL INSTRUCTION If a student scores below 3 for a skill, use the recommendations below to provide additional instruction for the skill.

RATE

If...	a student scores fewer than 40 wpm on this passage,
then...	identify reading rate difficulties (repetitions, ineffective or slow decoding). Help the student correctly read miscues and eliminate repetitions within a paragraph and then reread the paragraph several times. To provide additional practice, use one of the Fluency Routines, 11–14.

ACCURACY

If...	a student's Record of Oral Reading indicates problems decoding specific word types,
then...	analyze the types of miscues made. Have the student reread a sentence with a miscued word. If the student is unable to decode the miscued word, model and teach how to decode those word types. Then have the student read these types of words in books at the student's reading level.

SUMMARIZE

If...	a student is unable to identify important ideas or details in this passage,
then...	model how to identify an important idea and the details that support it as you read aloud part of the passage. Then have the student do the same with the remainder of the passage. Use Routine 16, Summarizing, for additional instruction and practice.

COMPREHENSION Cause and Effect

If...	a student is unable to identify cause and effect in the text,
then...	explain that certain things cause other things to happen; e.g., your stomach growling (effect) because you are hungry (cause). Then, use the Cause and Effect graphic organizer (p. 123) to model how to record what causes daytime. Together with the student, record what causes nighttime.

VOCABULARY Compound Words

If...	a student has trouble identifying the meanings of compound words,
then...	explain that compound words are made up of two smaller words and often get their meaning from these smaller words. Model how to determine the meaning of *moonlight* based on the smaller words. Then help the student read these words and determine their meanings: *daytime, bedtime, toothbrush*.

WORD READING Compound Words

If...	a student has difficulty correctly reading compound words,
then...	use Routine 4, Word Parts Strategy, to provide instruction and practice reading the words *daytime, outside, everything, moonlight, bedtime, himself, anybody, football, inside, nighttime*.

Moving into Instruction 16

SUGGESTED SKILL INSTRUCTION If a student scores below 3 for a skill, use the recommendations below to provide additional instruction for the skill.

RATE

If...	a student scores fewer than 40 wpm on this passage,
then...	identify reading rate difficulties (repetitions, ineffective or slow decoding). Help the student correctly read miscues and eliminate repetitions within a paragraph and then reread the paragraph several times. To provide additional practice, use one of the Fluency Routines, 11–14.

ACCURACY

If...	a student's Record of Oral Reading indicates problems decoding specific word types,
then...	analyze the types of miscues made. Have the student reread a sentence with a miscued word. If the student is unable to decode the miscued word, model and teach how to decode those word types. Then have the student read these types of words in books at the student's reading level.

SUMMARIZE

If...	a student is unable to identify important ideas or details in this passage,
then...	model how to identify an important idea and the details that support it as you read aloud part of the passage. Then have the student do the same with the remainder of the passage. Use Routine 16, Summarizing, for additional instruction and practice.

COMPREHENSION Sequence

If...	a student is unable to identify sequence in this selection,
then...	read the first paragraph aloud and model how to identify (circle or highlight) the first clue words that signal sequence or time order *(long ago)*. Have the student read aloud the rest of the passage and help him or her identify other clue words *(then, today)* in the same manner.

VOCABULARY Antonyms

If...	a student has trouble identifying the meanings of antonyms,
then...	use the T-Chart graphic organizer (p. 125) and write *near* in the left column. Ask the student to read the word *near*, tell you what it means, and then say a word that has the opposite meaning. Write the antonym in the right column of the chart. Repeat with other words: *slow, big, flat*.

WORD READING Vowel Sounds of *y*

If...	a student has difficulty correctly reading words with the vowel sounds of *y*,
then...	use Routine 2, Whole-Word Blending, to provide instruction and practice reading the words *fly, sky, by, bunny, try, happy, my, funny, fry, kitty, cry*.

SUGGESTED SKILL INSTRUCTION If a student scores below 3 for a skill, use the recommendations below to provide additional instruction for the skill.

RATE	
If...	a student scores fewer than 45 wpm on this passage,
then...	identify reading rate difficulties (repetitions, ineffective or slow decoding). Help the student correctly read miscues and eliminate repetitions within a paragraph and then reread the paragraph several times. To provide additional practice, use one of the Fluency Routines, 11–14.

ACCURACY	
If...	a student's Record of Oral Reading indicates problems decoding specific word types,
then...	analyze the types of miscues made. Have the student reread a sentence with a miscued word. If the student is unable to decode the miscued word, model and teach how to decode those word types. Then have the student read these types of words in books at the student's reading level.

RETELL Character, Setting, and Plot	
If...	a student is unable to describe the characters, setting, or most important events in the plot,
then...	use the Character, Setting, and Plot graphic organizer (p. 120) or highlight words or phrases in the story to identify information about the characters, setting, or events. Then use Routine 15, Narrative Retelling, to model how to retell the important events in the plot.

COMPREHENSION Compare and Contrast	
If...	a student is unable to identify comparisons and contrasts in this selection,
then...	explain that when we compare and contrast two things, we tell how they are alike and how they are different. Reread the story together with the student, stopping at points to talk about and record how the girls' summers were alike and different using the Venn Diagram graphic organizer (p. 122).

VOCABULARY Context Clues	
If...	a student has trouble identifying and using context clues to determine the meanings of unknown words,
then...	read aloud the third paragraph and model how readers find words and phrases near a word *(lasso)* that provide clues to the meaning of the word. Then work with the student to figure out the meaning of other words, such as *cactus* or *ranch*.

WORD READING Syllable Pattern VC/CV	
If...	a student has difficulty correctly reading words with the VC/CV syllable pattern,
then...	use Routine 4, Word Parts Strategy, to provide instruction and practice reading the words *rabbits, lasso, cactus, forget, contest, sister, magnet, number.*

Moving into Instruction 16

SUGGESTED SKILL INSTRUCTION If a student scores below 3 for a skill, use the recommendations below to provide additional instruction for the skill.

RATE

If...	a student scores fewer than 55 wpm on this passage,
then...	identify reading rate difficulties (repetitions, ineffective or slow decoding). Help the student correctly read miscues and eliminate repetitions within a paragraph and then reread the paragraph several times. To provide additional practice, use one of the Fluency Routines, 11–14.

ACCURACY

If...	a student's Record of Oral Reading indicates problems decoding specific word types,
then...	analyze the types of miscues made. Have the student reread a sentence with a miscued word. If the student is unable to decode the miscued word, model and teach how to decode those word types. Then have the student read these types of words in books at the student's reading level.

RETELL Character, Setting, and Plot

If...	a student is unable to describe the characters, setting, or most important events in the plot,
then...	use the Character, Setting, and Plot graphic organizer (p. 120) or highlight words or phrases in the story to identify information about the characters, setting, or events. Then use Routine 15, Narrative Retelling, to model how to retell the important events in the plot.

COMPREHENSION Compare and Contrast

If...	a student is unable to identify comparisons and contrasts in this story,
then...	have the student reread the story aloud. Work together to compare and contrast the features of the first three boxes and the last box that Pam opens. Record the differences and similarities on a Venn Diagram graphic organizer (p. 122).

VOCABULARY Context Clues

If...	a student has trouble identifying and using context clues to determine the meanings of words,
then...	point out specific words and phrases that provide clues to the unknown word *heavy*, such as "she tries to pick it up." Then help the student figure out the meaning of the word *tiny* by finding words or phrases that provide clues to its meaning.

WORD READING Comparative Word Endings *-er* and *-est*

If...	a student has difficulty correctly reading words with comparative endings,
then...	use Routine 4, Word Parts Strategy, to provide instruction and practice reading the words *tinier, tiniest, heaviest, heavier, funnier, funniest, happier, happiest, sunnier, sunniest.*

SUGGESTED SKILL INSTRUCTION If a student scores below 3 for a skill, use the recommendations below to provide additional instruction for the skill.

RATE

If...	a student scores fewer than 55 wpm on this passage,
then...	identify reading rate difficulties (repetitions, ineffective or slow decoding). Help the student correctly read miscues and eliminate repetitions within a paragraph and then reread the paragraph several times. To provide additional practice, use one of the Fluency Routines, 11–14.

ACCURACY

If...	a student's Record of Oral Reading indicates problems decoding specific word types,
then...	analyze the types of miscues made. Have the student reread a sentence with a miscued word. If the student is unable to decode the miscued word, model and teach how to decode those word types. Then have the student read these types of words in books at the student's reading level.

RETELL Character, Setting, and Plot

If...	a student is unable to describe the characters, setting, or most important events in the plot,
then...	use the Character, Setting, and Plot graphic organizer (p. 120) or highlight words or phrases in the story to identify information about the characters, setting, or events. Then use Routine 15, Narrative Retelling, to model how to retell the important events in the plot.

COMPREHENSION Draw Conclusions

If...	a student is unable to draw conclusions about this selection,
then...	explain that we draw a conclusion when we put new information together with what we already know. Use the Draw Conclusions graphic organizer (p. 124) to model how to use information from the story to draw a conclusion about what Jon will tell Nick. Work with the student to draw other conclusions.

VOCABULARY Compound Words

If...	a student has trouble identifying the meanings of compound words,
then...	explain that the meaning of a compound word isn't always exactly related to its two smaller words. Using the word *someone*, explain that *some* means "unknown," and *one* refers to a person. *Someone* is "an unknown person." Help the student read these words and determine their meanings: *somewhere, sometime, anyone.*

WORD READING Compound Words

If...	a student has difficulty correctly reading compound words,
then...	use Routine 4, Word Parts Strategy, to provide instruction and practice reading the words *something, someone, everything, anywhere, moonlight, anything, everyone, doghouse, anyone.*

SUGGESTED SKILL INSTRUCTION If a student scores below 3 for a skill, use the recommendations below to provide additional instruction for the skill.

RATE	
If...	a student scores fewer than 50 wpm on this passage,
then...	identify reading rate difficulties (repetitions, ineffective or slow decoding). Help the student correctly read miscues and eliminate repetitions within a paragraph and then reread the paragraph several times. To provide additional practice, use one of the Fluency Routines, 11–14.

ACCURACY	
If...	a student's Record of Oral Reading indicates problems decoding specific word types,
then...	analyze the types of miscues made. Have the student reread a sentence with a miscued word. If the student is unable to decode the miscued word, model and teach how to decode those word types. Then have the student read these types of words in books at the student's reading level.

SUMMARIZE	
If...	a student is unable to identify important ideas or details in this passage,
then...	model how to identify an important idea and the details that support it as you read aloud part of the passage. Then have the student do the same with the remainder of the passage. Use Routine 16, Summarizing, for additional instruction and practice.

COMPREHENSION Compare and Contrast	
If...	a student is unable to compare and contrast information in this selection,
then...	explain that when we compare and contrast two things, we tell how they are alike and how they are different. Reread the story with the student, stopping at points to talk about and record how the two flags were alike and different on a Venn Diagram graphic organizer (p. 122).

VOCABULARY Synonyms	
If...	a student cannot identify synonyms for words in the selection,
then...	use the T-Chart graphic organizer (p. 125) and write *fast* and *finish* in the left column. Ask the student to read each word, tell you what it means, and then say another word that has the same meaning. Write the synonyms in the right column of the chart. Repeat with other words: *began, drawing, happy.*

WORD READING Irregular High-Frequency Words	
If...	a student has difficulty correctly reading irregular high-frequency words,
then...	use Routine 8, Nondecodable Words Strategy, to provide instruction and practice reading the words *who, people, would, look, also, good, one, wanted, have, could, was, very.*

SUGGESTED SKILL INSTRUCTION If a student scores below 3 for a skill, use the recommendations below to provide additional instruction for the skill.

RATE

If...	a student scores fewer than 50 wpm on this passage,
then...	identify reading rate difficulties (repetitions, ineffective or slow decoding). Help the student correctly read miscues and eliminate repetitions within a paragraph and then reread the paragraph several times. To provide additional practice, use one of the Fluency Routines, 11–14.

ACCURACY

If...	a student's Record of Oral Reading indicates problems decoding specific word types,
then...	analyze the types of miscues made. Have the student reread a sentence with a miscued word. If the student is unable to decode the miscued word, model and teach how to decode those word types. Then have the student read these types of words in books at the student's reading level.

SUMMARIZE

If...	a student is unable to summarize the information in this selection,
then...	model how to identify an important idea and the details that support it as you read aloud part of the passage. Then have the student do the same with the remainder of the passage. Use Routine 16, Summarizing, for additional instruction and practice.

COMPREHENSION Draw Conclusions

If...	a student is unable to draw conclusions about this selection,
then...	explain that we draw a conclusion about things when we put new information together with what we already know. Reread the passage. Think aloud using information from the passage to draw a conclusion about the Pilgrims' first year in America. Then work with the student to draw other conclusions.

VOCABULARY Multiple-Meaning Words

If...	a student cannot identify the correct meanings of one of the multiple-meaning words in the selection,
then...	model using different definitions of the word *hard* (not easy; not soft) in context. Discuss which definition makes the most sense in this passage. Help the student use this method to determine the correct meanings of the words *waves* and *trip*.

WORD READING Long Vowel Digraphs *ow, igh, ew, ue*

If...	a student has difficulty correctly reading words with these long vowel digraphs,
then...	use Routine 2, Whole-Word Blending, to provide instruction and practice reading the words *grow, high, new, blue, sigh, low, few, Sue, mow, dew, light*.

Moving into Instruction **18**

SUGGESTED SKILL INSTRUCTION If a student scores below 3 for a skill, use the recommendations below to provide additional instruction for the skill.

RATE

If...	a student scores fewer than 65 wpm on this passage,
then...	identify reading rate difficulties (repetitions, ineffective or slow decoding). Help the student correctly read miscues and eliminate repetitions within a paragraph and then reread the paragraph several times. To provide additional practice, use one of the Fluency Routines, 11–14.

ACCURACY

If...	a student's Record of Oral Reading indicates problems decoding specific word types,
then...	analyze the types of miscues made. Have the student reread a sentence with a miscued word. If the student is unable to decode the miscued word, model and teach how to decode those word types. Then have the student read these types of words in books at the student's reading level.

RETELL Character, Setting, and Plot

If...	a student is unable to describe the characters, setting, or most important events in the plot,
then...	use the Character, Setting, and Plot graphic organizer (p. 120) or highlight words or phrases in the story to identify information about the characters, setting, or events. Then use Routine 15, Narrative Retelling, to model how to retell the important events in the plot.

COMPREHENSION Compare and Contrast

If...	a student is unable to identify comparisons and contrasts in this story,
then...	explain that when we compare and contrast two things, we tell how they are alike and how they are different. Have the student read aloud the two paragraphs about Sue and Kathy. Together record how the girls' desires are similar and different on a Venn Diagram graphic organizer (p. 122).

VOCABULARY Multiple-Meaning Words

If...	a student cannot identify the correct meanings for the multiple-meaning words in the selection,
then...	model using different definitions of the word *watch* (to look, see, observe; an instrument for keeping time) in context. Discuss which definition makes the most sense in this passage. Help the student use this method to determine the correct meanings of the words *class* and *play*.

WORD READING Long and Short Vowels, Consonant Blends, Digraphs

If...	a student has difficulty correctly reading words with long and short vowels, consonant blends, and digraphs,
then...	use Routine 3, Vowel-First Blending, to provide instruction and practice reading the words *Tim, time, plan, plane, class, beat, hop, hope, rip, ripe, heat, meek, stop, grass*.

SUGGESTED SKILL INSTRUCTION If a student scores below 3 for a skill, use the recommendations below to provide additional instruction for the skill.

RATE

If...	a student scores fewer than 60 wpm on this passage,
then...	identify reading rate difficulties (repetitions, ineffective or slow decoding). Help the student correctly read miscues and eliminate repetitions within a paragraph and then reread the paragraph several times. To provide additional practice, use one of the Fluency Routines, 11–14.

ACCURACY

If...	a student's Record of Oral Reading indicates problems decoding specific word types,
then...	analyze the types of miscues made. Have the student reread a sentence with a miscued word. If the student is unable to decode the miscued word, model and teach how to decode those word types. Then have the student read these types of words in books at the student's reading level.

SUMMARIZE

If...	a student is unable to identify important ideas or details in this passage,
then...	model how to identify an important idea and the details that support it as you read aloud part of the passage. Then have the student do the same with the remainder of the passage. Use Routine 16, Summarizing, for additional instruction and practice.

COMPREHENSION Compare and Contrast

If...	a student is unable to identify comparisons and contrasts in this passage,
then...	explain that when we compare and contrast two things, we tell how they are alike and how they are different. Have the student read aloud the second and third paragraphs. Together record how the slide and the seesaw are alike and different on a Venn Diagram graphic organizer (p. 122).

VOCABULARY Context Clues

If...	a student has trouble identifying and using context clues to determine the meanings of words,
then...	point out specific words and phrases that provide clues to the unknown word *inclined*, such as "the steps and the slide are... inclined planes." Then help the student figure out meanings of the words *shovel* and *machines* by finding words or phrases that provide clues to their meanings.

WORD READING *r*-Controlled Vowels

If...	a student has difficulty correctly reading words with *r*-controlled vowels,
then...	use Routine 1, Sound-by-Sound Blending, to provide instruction and practice reading the words *girl, park, car, jar, dark, sharp, bird, dirt, sport, north, park, cord, born.*

Moving into Instruction **20**

SUGGESTED SKILL INSTRUCTION If a student scores below 3 for a skill, use the recommendations below to provide additional instruction for the skill.

RATE	
If...	a student scores fewer than 65 wpm on this passage,
then...	identify reading rate difficulties (repetitions, ineffective or slow decoding). Help the student correctly read miscues and eliminate repetitions within a paragraph and then reread the paragraph several times. To provide additional practice, use one of the Fluency Routines, 11–14.

ACCURACY	
If...	a student's Record of Oral Reading indicates problems decoding specific word types,
then...	analyze the types of miscues made. Have the student reread a sentence with a miscued word. If the student is unable to decode the miscued word, model and teach how to decode those word types. Then have the student read these types of words in books at the student's reading level.

RETELL Character, Setting, and Plot	
If...	a student is unable to describe the characters, setting, or most important events in the plot,
then...	use the Character, Setting, and Plot graphic organizer (p. 120) or highlight words or phrases in the story to identify information about the characters, setting, or events. Then use Routine 15, Narrative Retelling, to model how to retell the important events in the plot.

COMPREHENSION Draw Conclusions	
If...	a student is unable to draw conclusions from this passage,
then...	explain that we draw a conclusion about things when we put new information together with what we already know. Use the Draw Conclusions graphic organizer (p. 124) to model using information from the story to draw a conclusion about what kind of cake Ben's friends made. Work with the student to draw other conclusions.

VOCABULARY Antonyms	
If...	a student has trouble identifying the meanings of antonyms,
then...	use the T-Chart graphic organizer (p. 125) and write *sad* in the left column. Ask the student to read the word and tell you what *sad* means, and then have the student say a word that has the opposite meaning. Write the antonym in the right column of the chart. Repeat with other words: *outside, opened, started.*

WORD READING Syllable Pattern VC/CV	
If...	a student has difficulty correctly reading words with the VC/CV syllable pattern,
then...	use Routine 4, Word Parts Strategy, to provide instruction and practice reading the words *party, market, carton, carrots, butter, entire, magnet, pencil, basket, garden, rabbit, window.*

SUGGESTED SKILL INSTRUCTION If a student scores below 3 for a skill, use the recommendations below to provide additional instruction for the skill.

RATE

If...	a student scores fewer than 60 wpm on this passage,
then...	identify reading rate difficulties (repetitions, ineffective or slow decoding). Help the student correctly read miscues and eliminate repetitions within a paragraph and then reread the paragraph several times. To provide additional practice, use one of the Fluency Routines, 11–14.

ACCURACY

If...	a student's Record of Oral Reading indicates problems decoding specific word types,
then...	analyze the types of miscues made. Have the student reread a sentence with a miscued word. If the student is unable to decode the miscued word, model and teach how to decode those word types. Then have the student read these types of words in books at the student's reading level.

SUMMARIZE

If...	a student is unable to identify important ideas or details in this passage,
then...	model how to identify an important idea and the details that support it as you read aloud part of the passage. Then have the student do the same with the remainder of the passage. Use Routine 16, Summarizing, for additional instruction and practice.

COMPREHENSION Cause and Effect

If...	a student is unable to identify cause and effect in the text,
then...	explain that certain things cause other things to happen; e.g., you wear a coat (effect) because it's cold outside (cause). Then, using the Cause and Effect graphic organizer (p. 123), model how to find out and record what makes new soil. Together with the student, record other causes and effects.

VOCABULARY Synonyms

If...	a student has trouble identifying synonyms,
then...	use the T-Chart graphic organizer (p. 125) and write *gift* and *soil* in the left column. Ask the student to read each word and tell you what it means, and then say another word that has the same meaning. Write the synonyms in the right column of the chart. Repeat with other words: *nap, build, things.*

WORD READING Contractions

If...	a student has difficulty correctly reading words with contractions,
then...	use Routine 1, Sound-by-Sound Blending, to provide instruction and practice reading the words *we're, we've, we'll, she'll, I'll, you've, I've, you're.*

Moving into Instruction 20

SUGGESTED SKILL INSTRUCTION If a student scores below 3 for a skill, use the recommendations below to provide additional instruction for the skill.

RATE

If...	a student scores fewer than 65 wpm on this passage,
then...	identify reading rate difficulties (repetitions, ineffective or slow decoding). Help the student correctly read miscues and eliminate repetitions within a paragraph and then reread the paragraph several times. To provide additional practice, use one of the Fluency Routines, 11–14.

ACCURACY

If...	a student's Record of Oral Reading indicates problems decoding specific word types,
then...	analyze the types of miscues made. Have the student reread a sentence with a miscued word. If the student is unable to decode the miscued word, model and teach how to decode those word types. Then have the student read these types of words in books at the student's reading level.

RETELL Character, Setting, and Plot

If...	a student is unable to describe the characters, setting, or most important events in the plot,
then...	use the Character, Setting, and Plot graphic organizer (p. 120) or highlight words or phrases in the story to identify information about the characters, setting, or events. Then use Routine 15, Narrative Retelling, to model how to retell the important events in the plot.

COMPREHENSION Sequence

If...	a student is unable to identify sequence in this story,
then...	read aloud the fifth paragraph and model how to identify (circle or highlight) the first clue word that signals sequence. Help the student identify the other clue words in the paragraph.

VOCABULARY Context Clues

If...	a student has trouble identifying and using context clues to determine the meanings of words,
then...	point out specific words and phrases that provide clues to the unknown word *molds*, such as "special molds to shape the cheese." Then help the student figure out the meaning of the word *hungry* by finding words or phrases that provide clues to its meaning.

WORD READING Vowel Diphthongs

If...	a student has difficulty correctly reading words with vowel diphthongs,
then...	use Routine 2, Whole-Word Blending, to provide instruction and practice reading the words *mouse, soil, cows, now, around, brown, ouch, yawn, draw, voice, enjoy, point, mouth.*

SUGGESTED SKILL INSTRUCTION If a student scores below 3 for a skill, use the recommendations below to provide additional instruction for the skill.

RATE

If...	a student scores fewer than 70 wpm on this passage,
then...	identify reading rate difficulties (repetitions, ineffective or slow decoding). Help the student correctly read miscues and eliminate repetitions within a paragraph and then reread the paragraph several times. To provide additional practice, use one of the Fluency Routines, 11–14.

ACCURACY

If...	a student's Record of Oral Reading indicates problems decoding specific word types,
then...	analyze the types of miscues made. Have the student reread a sentence with a miscued word. If the student is unable to decode the miscued word, model and teach how to decode those word types. Then have the student read these types of words in books at the student's reading level.

RETELL Character, Setting, and Plot

If...	a student is unable to describe the characters, setting, or most important events in the plot,
then...	use the Character, Setting, and Plot graphic organizer (p. 120) or highlight words or phrases in the story to identify information about the characters, setting, or events. Then use Routine 15, Narrative Retelling, to model how to retell the important events in the plot.

COMPREHENSION Sequence

If...	a student is unable to identify sequence in this story,
then...	highlight the word *July* and explain that months, time of the year, or time of day can all indicate sequence. Have the student read aloud and identify (circle or highlight) the other clue words/phrases that signal sequence.

VOCABULARY Multiple-Meaning Words

If...	a student cannot identify the correct meanings for the multiple-meaning words in the selection,
then...	model using different definitions of the word *hard* (difficult to do; solid, firm) in context. Discuss which definition makes the most sense in this passage. Help the student use this method to determine the correct meanings of the words *box, back,* and *hand.*

WORD READING Syllable Patterns V/CV and VC/V

If...	a student has difficulty correctly reading words with these syllable patterns,
then...	use Routine 4, Word Parts Strategy, to provide instruction and practice reading the words *July, baby, present, photo, baker, cabin, comic, music, sofa, tiger, shiver.*

Moving into Instruction **24**

SUGGESTED SKILL INSTRUCTION If a student scores below 3 for a skill, use the recommendations below to provide additional instruction for the skill.

RATE

If...	a student scores fewer than 65 wpm on this passage,
then...	identify reading rate difficulties (repetitions, ineffective or slow decoding). Help the student correctly read miscues and eliminate repetitions within a paragraph and then reread the paragraph several times. To provide additional practice, use one of the Fluency Routines, 11–14.

ACCURACY

If...	a student's Record of Oral Reading indicates problems decoding specific word types,
then...	analyze the types of miscues made. Have the student reread a sentence with a miscued word. If the student is unable to decode the miscued word, model and teach how to decode those word types. Then have the student read these types of words in books at the student's reading level.

SUMMARIZE

If...	a student is unable to identify important ideas or details in this passage,
then...	model how to identify an important idea and the details that support it as you read aloud part of the passage. Then have the student do the same with the remainder of the passage. Use Routine 16, Summarizing, for additional instruction and practice.

COMPREHENSION Cause and Effect

If...	a student is unable to identify cause and effect in the text,
then...	use the Cause and Effect graphic organizer (p. 123) to model how to find out and record why something happened *(decided to trade because he didn't have the money)*. Together with the student, list other causes and effects. Remind the student that a cause-and-effect relationship consists of what happened and why.

VOCABULARY Synonyms

If...	a student has trouble identifying synonyms,
then...	use the T-Chart graphic organizer (p. 125) and write *trade* and *shaped* in the left column. Ask the student to read each word and tell you what it means, and then say another word that has the same meaning. Write the synonyms in the right column of the chart. Repeat with the words *house* and *thought*.

WORD READING Vowel Patterns *aw, au, al*

If...	a student has difficulty correctly reading words with these vowel patterns,
then...	use Routine 2, Whole-Word Blending, to provide instruction and practice reading the words *walk, caught, saw, talking, yawn, chalk, crawl, Paul, sauce*.

SUGGESTED SKILL INSTRUCTION If a student scores below 3 for a skill, use the recommendations below to provide additional instruction for the skill.

RATE

If...	a student scores fewer than 70 wpm on this passage,
then...	identify reading rate difficulties (repetitions, ineffective or slow decoding). Help the student correctly read miscues and eliminate repetitions within a paragraph and then reread the paragraph several times. To provide additional practice, use one of the Fluency Routines, 11–14.

ACCURACY

If...	a student's Record of Oral Reading indicates problems decoding specific word types,
then...	analyze the types of miscues made. Have the student reread a sentence with a miscued word. If the student is unable to decode the miscued word, model and teach how to decode those word types. Then have the student read these types of words in books at the student's reading level.

RETELL Character, Setting, and Plot

If...	a student is unable to describe the characters, setting, or most important events in the plot,
then...	use the Character, Setting, and Plot graphic organizer (p. 120) or highlight words or phrases in the story to identify information about the characters, setting, or events. Then use Routine 15, Narrative Retelling, to model how to retell the important events in the plot.

COMPREHENSION Cause and Effect

If...	a student is unable to identify cause and effect in the text,
then...	use the Cause and Effect graphic organizer (p. 123) to model finding out and recording why something happened (didn't go to the park...too hot). Together with the student, list other causes and effects. Remind the student that a cause-and-effect relationship consists of what happened and why.

VOCABULARY Compound Words

If...	a student has trouble identifying the meanings of compound words,
then...	use the word *summertime* to explain that *summertime* is the time, or season, of summer. Sometimes we can use the two smaller words in a compound word to determine its meaning. Have the student explain the meanings of *dinnertime* and *notepad* in a similar way.

WORD READING Compound Words

If...	a student has difficulty correctly reading compound words,
then...	use Routine 4, Word Parts Strategy, to provide instruction and practice reading the words *cleanup, afternoon, something, sidewalk, ladybug, without, daytime, popcorn, nobody*.

Moving into Instruction **24**

SUGGESTED SKILL INSTRUCTION If a student scores below 3 for a skill, use the recommendations below to provide additional instruction for the skill.

RATE

If...	a student scores fewer than 65 wpm on this passage,
then...	identify reading rate difficulties (repetitions, ineffective or slow decoding). Help the student correctly read miscues and eliminate repetitions within a paragraph and then reread the paragraph several times. To provide additional practice, use one of the Fluency Routines, 11–14.

ACCURACY

If...	a student's Record of Oral Reading indicates problems decoding specific word types,
then...	analyze the types of miscues made. Have the student reread a sentence with a miscued word. If the student is unable to decode the miscued word, model and teach how to decode those word types. Then have the student read these types of words in books at the student's reading level.

SUMMARIZE

If...	a student is unable to identify important ideas or details in this passage,
then...	model how to identify an important idea and the details that support it as you read aloud part of the passage. Then have the student do the same with the remainder of the passage. Use Routine 16, Summarizing, for additional instruction and practice.

COMPREHENSION Compare and Contrast

If...	a student is unable to identify comparisons and contrasts in this passage,
then...	together reread the passage and highlight clue words for comparisons and contrasts, such as *different* and *both*. Then help the student record how turtles and tortoises are similar and different on a Venn Diagram graphic organizer (p. 122).

VOCABULARY Compound Words

If...	a student has trouble identifying the meanings of compound words,
then...	use the word *wildflowers* to explain that a *wildflower* is a flower that grows in the wild. Sometimes we can use the two smaller words in a compound word to determine its meaning. Help the student read the following words and then determine their meanings: *dinnertime, backpack,* and *moonlight.*

WORD READING Consonant Blends

If...	a student has difficulty correctly reading words with consonant blends,
then...	use Routine 3, Vowel-First Blending, to provide instruction and practice reading the words *stumps, spend, plants, grass, cloud, stone, plant, snail, milk, desk, drop.*

SUGGESTED SKILL INSTRUCTION If a student scores below 3 for a skill, use the recommendations below to provide additional instruction for the skill.

RATE

If...	a student scores fewer than 65 wpm on this passage,
then...	identify reading rate difficulties (repetitions, ineffective or slow decoding). Help the student correctly read miscues and eliminate repetitions within a paragraph and then reread the paragraph several times. To provide additional practice, use one of the Fluency Routines, 11–14.

ACCURACY

If...	a student's Record of Oral Reading indicates problems decoding specific word types,
then...	analyze the types of miscues made. Have the student reread a sentence with a miscued word. If the student is unable to decode the miscued word, model and teach how to decode those word types. Then have the student read these types of words in books at the student's reading level.

SUMMARIZE

If...	a student is unable to identify important ideas or details in this passage,
then...	model how to identify an important idea and the details that support it as you read aloud part of the passage. Then have the student do the same with the remainder of the passage. Use Routine 16, Summarizing, for additional instruction and practice.

COMPREHENSION Draw Conclusions

If...	a student is unable to draw conclusions from this selection,
then...	explain that we draw a conclusion when we put new information together with what we already know. Use the Draw Conclusions graphic organizer (p. 124) to model how to use information from the passage to draw a conclusion about the dwarf planet Pluto. Work with the student to draw other conclusions.

VOCABULARY Antonyms

If...	a student has trouble identifying the meanings of antonyms,
then...	use the T-Chart graphic organizer (p. 125) and write *different* in the left column. Ask the student to read the word and tell you what it means, and then have him or her say a word that has the opposite meaning. Write the antonym in the right column of the chart. Repeat with other words: *wrong, hotter, closer.*

WORD READING Silent Consonants

If...	a student has difficulty correctly reading words with silent consonants,
then...	use Routine 2, Whole-Word Blending, to provide instruction and practice reading the words *signs, know, write, wrong, gnat, thumb, lamb, knee, knot.*

Moving into Instruction **24**

SUGGESTED SKILL INSTRUCTION If a student scores below 3 for a skill, use the recommendations below to provide additional instruction for the skill.

RATE

If...	a student scores fewer than 75 wpm on this passage,
then...	identify reading rate difficulties (repetitions, ineffective or slow decoding). Help the student correctly read miscues and eliminate repetitions within a paragraph and then reread the paragraph several times. To provide additional practice, use one of the Fluency Routines, 11–14.

ACCURACY

If...	a student's Record of Oral Reading indicates problems decoding specific word types,
then...	analyze the types of miscues made. Have the student reread a sentence with a miscued word. If the student is unable to decode the miscued word, model and teach how to decode those word types. Then have the student read these types of words in books at the student's reading level.

RETELL Character, Setting, and Plot

If...	a student is unable to describe the characters, setting, or most important events in the plot,
then...	use the Character, Setting, and Plot graphic organizer (p. 120) or highlight words or phrases in the story to identify information about the characters, setting, or events. Then use Routine 15, Narrative Retelling, to model how to retell the important events in the plot.

COMPREHENSION Sequence

If...	a student is unable to identify sequence in this story,
then...	begin reading the story aloud and model how to identify (circle or highlight) the first clue word that signals sequence *(when)*. Have the student read the rest of the story aloud and identify other clue words.

VOCABULARY Multiple-Meaning Words

If...	a student cannot identify the correct meanings for the multiple-meaning words in the selection,
then...	model using different definitions of the word *leaves* (goes away; parts of plants) in context. Discuss which definition makes the most sense in this passage. Help the student use this method to determine the correct meanings of the words *ground*, *feet*, and *saw*.

WORD READING Irregular High-Frequency Words

If...	a student has difficulty correctly reading irregular high-frequency words,
then...	use Routine 8, Nondecodable Words Strategy, to provide instruction and practice reading the words *afraid, ahead, watch, special, noticed, people, water, answer, enough, guess, where, early, country.*

SUGGESTED SKILL INSTRUCTION If a student scores below 3 for a skill, use the recommendations below to provide additional instruction for the skill.

RATE

If...	a student scores fewer than 70 wpm on this passage,
then...	identify reading rate difficulties (repetitions, ineffective or slow decoding). Help the student correctly read miscues and eliminate repetitions within a paragraph and then reread the paragraph several times. To provide additional practice, use one of the Fluency Routines, 11–14.

ACCURACY

If...	a student's Record of Oral Reading indicates problems decoding specific word types,
then...	analyze the types of miscues made. Have the student reread a sentence with a miscued word. If the student is unable to decode the miscued word, model and teach how to decode those word types. Then have the student read these types of words in books at the student's reading level.

SUMMARIZE

If...	a student is unable to identify important ideas or details in this passage,
then...	model how to identify an important idea and the details that support it as you read aloud part of the passage. Then have the student do the same with the remainder of the passage. Use Routine 16, Summarizing, for additional instruction and practice.

COMPREHENSION Sequence

If...	a student is unable to identify sequence in this story,
then...	read aloud the first paragraph and model how to identify (circle or highlight) the first clue word that signals sequence *(first)*. Have the student identify the other signal word *(then)*. Reread the last paragraph and think aloud, showing how the reader must sometimes assume a sequence of events.

VOCABULARY Synonyms

If...	a student has trouble identifying synonyms,
then...	use the T-Chart graphic organizer (p. 125) and write *adult* and *explains* in the left column. Ask the student to read each word and tell you what it means, and then say another word that has the same meaning. Write the synonyms in the right column of the chart. Repeat with the words *pick* and *excellent*.

WORD READING Consonant + *le*

If...	a student has difficulty correctly reading words with consonants + *le*,
then...	use Routine 4, Word Parts Strategy, to provide instruction and practice reading the words *possible*, *struggle*, *able*, *people*, *bubble*, *purple*, *uncle*, *table*, *handle*.

Moving into Instruction **28**

SUGGESTED SKILL INSTRUCTION If a student scores below 3 for a skill, use the recommendations below to provide additional instruction for the skill.

RATE

If...	a student scores fewer than 75 wpm on this passage,
then...	identify reading rate difficulties (repetitions, ineffective or slow decoding). Help the student correctly read miscues and eliminate repetitions within a paragraph and then reread the paragraph several times. To provide additional practice, use one of the Fluency Routines, 11–14.

ACCURACY

If...	a student's Record of Oral Reading indicates problems decoding specific word types,
then...	analyze the types of miscues made. Have the student reread a sentence with a miscued word. If the student is unable to decode the miscued word, model and teach how to decode those word types. Then have the student read these types of words in books at the student's reading level.

RETELL Character, Setting, and Plot

If...	a student is unable to describe the characters, setting, or most important events in the plot,
then...	use the Character, Setting, and Plot graphic organizer (p. 120) or highlight words or phrases in the story to identify information about the characters, setting, or events. Then use Routine 15, Narrative Retelling, to model how to retell the important events in the plot.

COMPREHENSION Draw Conclusions

If...	a student is unable to draw conclusions from this selection,
then...	explain that we draw a conclusion about things when we put new information together with what we already know. Use the Draw Conclusions graphic organizer (p. 124) to model how to use information from the passage to draw a conclusion about why Joe woke up. Work with the student to draw other conclusions.

VOCABULARY Antonyms

If...	a student has trouble identifying the meanings of antonyms,
then...	use the T-Chart graphic organizer (p. 125) and write *over* in the left column. Ask the student to read the word and tell you what it means, and then have the student say a word that has the opposite meaning. Then write the antonym in the right column of the chart. Repeat with other words: *quickly, follow, behind.*

WORD READING Short and Long Vowels

If...	a student has difficulty correctly reading words with short and long vowels,
then...	use Routine 2, Whole-Word Blending, to provide instruction and practice reading the words *woke, like, planet, went, with, rock, time, apple, best, nice, pick, ate, even, must, use, note, dot.*

Moving into Instruction 28

SUGGESTED SKILL INSTRUCTION If a student scores below 3 for a skill, use the recommendations below to provide additional instruction for the skill.

RATE

If...	a student scores fewer than 70 wpm on this passage,
then...	identify reading rate difficulties (repetitions, ineffective or slow decoding). Help the student correctly read miscues and eliminate repetitions within a paragraph and then reread the paragraph several times. To provide additional practice, use one of the Fluency Routines, 11–14.

ACCURACY

If...	a student's Record of Oral Reading indicates problems decoding specific word types,
then...	analyze the types of miscues made. Have the student reread a sentence with a miscued word. If the student is unable to decode the miscued word, model and teach how to decode those word types. Then have the student read these types of words in books at the student's reading level.

SUMMARIZE

If...	a student is unable to identify important ideas or details in this passage,
then...	model how to identify an important idea and the details that support it as you read aloud part of the passage. Then have the student do the same with the remainder of the passage. Use Routine 16, Summarizing, for additional instruction and practice.

COMPREHENSION Cause and Effect

If...	a student is unable to identify cause and effect in the text,
then...	use the Cause and Effect graphic organizer (p. 123) to model how to find out and record what happens when you drop a ball. Together with the student, list some of the effects of living with and without gravity. Remind the student that a cause-and-effect relationship consists of what happened and why.

VOCABULARY Prefixes

If...	a student has trouble identifying prefixes,
then...	write the words *return* and *unhappy*. Explain that the prefix *re-* means "again," so the word *return* means "to turn again." Help the student determine the meaning of the prefix *un-* and the word *unhappy*. Ask him or her to use each word in a sentence. Repeat with other words: *unable, undo, reread, repaint*.

WORD READING Prefixes

If...	a student has difficulty correctly reading words with prefixes,
then...	use Routine 4, Word Parts Strategy, to provide instruction and practice reading the words *return, dislike, unhappy, repay, disorder, reuse, unkind*.

Moving into Instruction 28

SUGGESTED SKILL INSTRUCTION If a student scores below 3 for a skill, use the recommendations below to provide additional instruction for the skill.

RATE

If...	a student scores fewer than 75 wpm on this passage,
then...	identify reading rate difficulties (repetitions, ineffective or slow decoding). Help the student correctly read miscues and eliminate repetitions within a paragraph and then reread the paragraph several times. To provide additional practice, use one of the Fluency Routines, 11–14.

ACCURACY

If...	a student's Record of Oral Reading indicates problems decoding specific word types,
then...	analyze the types of miscues made. Have the student reread a sentence with a miscued word. If the student is unable to decode the miscued word, model and teach how to decode those word types. Then have the student read these types of words in books at the student's reading level.

RETELL Character, Setting, and Plot

If...	a student is unable to describe the characters, setting, or most important events in the plot,
then...	use the Character, Setting, and Plot graphic organizer (p. 120) or highlight words or phrases in the story to identify information about the characters, setting, or events. Then use Routine 15, Narrative Retelling, to model how to retell the important events in the plot.

COMPREHENSION Compare and Contrast

If...	a student is unable to identify comparisons and contrasts in this story,
then...	have the student read aloud the second through fifth paragraphs. Together, identify and record on a Venn Diagram graphic organizer (p. 122) how the two cards were made. Call the student's attention to the author's use of descriptive words such as *skillfully, careful, quickly, slowly, wordless*.

VOCABULARY Suffixes

If...	a student has trouble identifying word meanings using suffixes,
then...	write the words *careful* and *wordless*. Explain that the suffix *-ful* means "full of," so the word *careful* means "full of care." Help the student determine the meaning of the suffix *-less* and the word *wordless*. Ask him or her to use each word in a sentence. Repeat with other words: *hopeless, helpful, beautiful*.

WORD READING Suffixes

If...	a student has difficulty correctly reading words with suffixes,
then...	use Routine 4, Word Parts Strategy, to provide instruction and practice reading the words *beautiful, careless, goodness, quickly, careful, wordless, kindness, slowly, helpful, colorful, darkness*.

Moving into Instruction **28**

SUGGESTED SKILL INSTRUCTION If a student scores below 3 for a skill, use the recommendations below to provide additional instruction for the skill.

RATE

If...	a student scores fewer than 75 wpm on this passage,
then...	identify reading rate difficulties (repetitions, ineffective or slow decoding). Help the student correctly read miscues and eliminate repetitions within a paragraph and then reread the paragraph several times. To provide additional practice, use one of the Fluency Routines, 11–14.

ACCURACY

If...	a student's Record of Oral Reading indicates problems decoding specific word types,
then...	analyze the types of miscues made. Have the student reread a sentence with a miscued word. If the student is unable to decode the miscued word, model and teach how to decode those word types. Then have the student read these types of words in books at the student's reading level.

SUMMARIZE

If...	a student is unable to identify important ideas or details in this passage,
then...	model how to identify an important idea and the details that support it as you read aloud part of the passage. Then have the student do the same with the remainder of the passage. Use Routine 16, Summarizing, for additional instruction and practice.

COMPREHENSION Draw Conclusions

If...	a student is unable to draw conclusions in this passage,
then...	explain that we draw a conclusion about things when we put new information together with what we already know. Use the Draw Conclusions graphic organizer (p. 124) to model using information from the passage to draw a conclusion about different kinds of communities. Work with the student to draw other conclusions.

VOCABULARY Multiple-Meaning Words

If...	a student cannot identify the correct meanings for the multiple-meaning words in the selection,
then...	model using different definitions of the word *can* (a metal container; able to do something) in context. Discuss which definition makes the most sense in this passage. Help the student use this method to determine the correct meanings of the words *pitcher* and *type*.

WORD READING Vowel Patterns *al, au, aw*

If...	a student has difficulty correctly reading words with these vowel patterns,
then...	use Routine 2, Whole-Word Blending, to provide instruction and practice reading the words *walking, baseball, haul, hawks, talked, brawl, salt, drawn, chalk.*

Moving into Instruction 30

SUGGESTED SKILL INSTRUCTION If a student scores below 3 for a skill, use the recommendations below to provide additional instruction for the skill.

RATE

If...	a student scores fewer than 80 wpm on this passage,
then...	identify reading rate difficulties (repetitions, ineffective or slow decoding). Help the student correctly read miscues and eliminate repetitions within a paragraph and then reread the paragraph several times. To provide additional practice, use one of the Fluency Routines, 11–14.

ACCURACY

If...	a student's Record of Oral Reading indicates problems decoding specific word types,
then...	analyze the types of miscues made. Have the student reread a sentence with a miscued word. If the student is unable to decode the miscued word, model and teach how to decode those word types. Then have the student read these types of words in books at the student's reading level.

RETELL Character, Setting, and Plot

If...	a student is unable to describe the characters, setting, or most important events in the plot,
then...	use the Character, Setting, and Plot graphic organizer (p. 120) or highlight words or phrases in the story to identify information about the characters, setting, or events. Then use Routine 15, Narrative Retelling, to model how to retell the important events in the plot.

COMPREHENSION Draw Conclusions

If...	a student is unable to draw conclusions in this selection,
then...	explain that we draw a conclusion when we put new information together with what we already know. Use the Draw Conclusions graphic organizer (p. 124) to model using information from the story to draw a conclusion about Mark's ability to take care of a pet. Work with the student to draw other conclusions.

VOCABULARY Antonyms

If...	a student has trouble identifying the meanings of antonyms,
then...	use the T-Chart graphic organizer (p. 125) and write *remember* in the left column. Ask the student to read the word and tell you what it means, and then have the student say a word that has the opposite meaning. Have the student write the antonym in the right column of the chart. Repeat with other words: *huge, later, wild, soft*.

WORD READING Syllable Patterns VC/CV and C + *le*

If...	a student has difficulty correctly reading words with these syllable patterns,
then...	use Routine 4, Word Parts Strategy, to provide instruction and practice reading the words *gerbil, perfect, bigger, eagle, turtle, little, expert, compute, luggage, tattle, battle, handle, fable*.

Moving into Instruction 30

SUGGESTED SKILL INSTRUCTION If a student scores below 3 for a skill, use the recommendations below to provide additional instruction for the skill.

RATE

If...	a student scores fewer than 75 wpm on this passage,
then...	identify reading rate difficulties (repetitions, ineffective or slow decoding). Help the student correctly read miscues and eliminate repetitions within a paragraph and then reread the paragraph several times. To provide additional practice, use one of the Fluency Routines, 11–14.

ACCURACY

If...	a student's Record of Oral Reading indicates problems decoding specific word types,
then...	analyze the types of miscues made. Have the student reread a sentence with a miscued word. If the student is unable to decode the miscued word, model and teach how to decode those word types. Then have the student read these types of words in books at the student's reading level.

SUMMARIZE

If...	a student is unable to identify important ideas or details in this passage,
then...	model at how to identify an important idea and the details that support it as you read aloud part of the passage. Then have the student do the same with the remainder of the passage. Use Routine 16, Summarizing, for additional instruction and practice.

COMPREHENSION Cause and Effect

If...	a student is unable to identify cause and effect in the text,
then...	use the Cause and Effect graphic organizer (p. 123) to model how to find out how cell phones keep people safe. Then have the student find out what happens when people using cell phones don't pay attention. Remind the student that a cause-and-effect relationship consists of what happened and why.

VOCABULARY Context Clues

If...	a student has trouble identifying word meanings using context clues,
then...	point out specific words and phrases that provide clues to the unknown word *rare*, such as "...few people owned cell phones. Having a cell phone was a rare treat." Then help the student figure out the meaning of the word *ignoring* by finding words or phrases that provide clues to its meaning.

WORD READING Base Words and Endings with Spelling Changes

If...	a student has difficulty correctly reading base words and endings with spelling changes,
then...	use Routine 4, Word Parts Strategy, to provide instruction and practice reading the words *having, ignoring, messaging, varied, preparing, supposing, funnier, scariest, angrily, easily, busier, messages*.

Moving into Instruction 30

SUGGESTED SKILL INSTRUCTION If a student scores below 3 for a skill, use the recommendations below to provide additional instruction for the skill.

RATE

If...	a student scores fewer than 80 wpm on this passage,
then...	identify reading rate difficulties (repetitions, ineffective or slow decoding). Help the student correctly read miscues and eliminate repetitions within a paragraph and then reread the paragraph several times. To provide additional practice, use one of the Fluency Routines, 11–14.

ACCURACY

If...	a student's Record of Oral Reading indicates problems decoding specific word types,
then...	analyze the types of miscues made. Have the student reread a sentence with a miscued word. If the student is unable to decode the miscued word, model and teach how to decode those word types. Then have the student read these types of words in books at the student's reading level.

RETELL Character, Setting, and Plot

If...	a student is unable to describe the characters, setting, or most important events in the plot,
then...	use the Character, Setting, and Plot graphic organizer (p. 120) or highlight words or phrases in the story to identify information about the characters, setting, or events. Then use Routine 15, Narrative Retelling, to model how to retell the important events in the plot.

COMPREHENSION Sequence

If...	a student is unable to identify sequence in this story,
then...	read aloud the fourth paragraph and model how to identify (circle or highlight) the first clue word that signals sequence *(today)*. Help the student identify another clue word *(then)*. Have the student read aloud the next paragraph and identify another sequence clue word *(next)*.

VOCABULARY Compound Words

If...	a student has trouble identifying the meanings of compound words,
then...	model how to cover each of the smaller words in the word *highchair* to figure out what each word means. Ask the student what *highchair* means. Then ask the student to use the same routine to determine the meaning of *blueberries*.

WORD READING Compound Words

If...	a student has difficulty correctly reading compound words,
then...	use Routine 4, Word Parts Strategy, to provide instruction and practice reading the words *toothbrush, blueberries, airplane, doorway, pigtail, sandpaper, eyebrow, handbag, backfield, barnyard, bedtime.*

Moving into Instruction 30

SUGGESTED SKILL INSTRUCTION If a student scores below 3 for a skill, use the recommendations below to provide additional instruction for the skill.

RATE	
If...	a student scores fewer than 75 wpm on this passage,
then...	identify reading rate difficulties (repetitions, ineffective or slow decoding). Help the student correctly read miscues and eliminate repetitions within a paragraph and then reread the paragraph several times. To provide additional practice, use one of the Fluency Routines, 11–14.

ACCURACY	
If...	a student's Record of Oral Reading indicates problems decoding specific word types,
then...	analyze the types of miscues made. Have the student reread a sentence with a miscued word. If the student is unable to decode the miscued word, model and teach how to decode those word types. Then have the student read these types of words in books at the student's reading level.

SUMMARIZE	
If...	a student is unable to identify important ideas or details in this passage,
then...	model how to identify an important idea and the details that support it as you read aloud part of the passage. Then have the student do the same with the remainder of the passage. Use Routine 16, Summarizing, for additional instruction and practice.

COMPREHENSION Compare and Contrast	
If...	a student is unable to identify comparisons and contrasts in this selection,
then...	explain that when we compare and contrast two things, we tell how they are alike and how they are different. Have the student read aloud the second and third paragraphs. Together identify and record on a Venn Diagram graphic organizer (p. 122) how living in a big city is similar to, yet different from, living in a small town.

VOCABULARY Synonyms	
If...	a student has trouble identifying synonyms,
then...	use the T-Chart graphic organizer (p. 125) and write *discover* and *anxious* in the left column. Ask the student to read each word and tell you what it means, and then say another word that has the same meaning. Write the synonyms in the right column of the chart. Repeat with other words: *larger, enjoy.*

WORD READING Multisyllabic Words	
If...	a student has difficulty correctly reading multisyllabic words,
then...	use Routine 6, Multisyllabic Word Strategy, to provide instruction and practice reading the words *experience, discover, probably, differences.*

Moving into Instruction **30**

SUGGESTED SKILL INSTRUCTION If a student scores below 3 for a skill, use the recommendations below to provide additional instruction for the skill.

RATE

If...	a student scores fewer than 85 wpm on this passage,
then...	identify reading rate difficulties (repetitions, ineffective or slow decoding). Help the student correctly read miscues and eliminate repetitions within a paragraph and then reread the paragraph several times. To provide additional practice, use one of the Fluency Routines, 11–14.

ACCURACY

If...	a student's Record of Oral Reading indicates problems decoding specific word types,
then...	analyze the types of miscues made. Have the student reread a sentence with a miscued word. If the student is unable to decode the miscued word, model and teach how to decode those word types. Then have the student read these types of words in books at the student's reading level.

RETELL Character, Setting, and Plot

If...	a student is unable to describe the characters, setting, or most important events in the plot,
then...	use the Character, Setting, and Plot graphic organizer (p. 120) or highlight words or phrases in the story to identify information about the characters, setting, or events. Then use Routine 15, Narrative Retelling, to model how to retell the important events in the plot.

COMPREHENSION Cause and Effect

If...	a student is unable to identify cause and effect in the text,
then...	use a Cause and Effect graphic organizer (p. 123) to model how to find why Katie falls asleep listening to the waves. Then have the student find what happened when Katharine Bates got to the top of Pikes Peak. Remind the student that a cause-and-effect relationship consists of what happened and why.

VOCABULARY Multiple-Meaning Words

If...	a student cannot identify the correct meanings for the multiple-meaning words in the selection,
then...	model using different definitions of the word *tear* (rip something; pull away from something) in context. Discuss which definition makes the most sense in this passage. Help the student use this method to determine the correct meanings of the words *cape*, *right*, and *call.*

WORD READING Consonant Digraphs *ph, gh, ch* /k/, *-dge* /j/

If...	a student has difficulty correctly reading words with these consonant digraphs,
then...	use Routine 2, Whole-Word Blending, to provide instruction and practice reading the words *phone, laughed, rough, school, edge, graph, badge, cough, dodge, photograph, lodge, enough.*

Moving into Instruction 34

SUGGESTED SKILL INSTRUCTION If a student scores below 3 for a skill, use the recommendations below to provide additional instruction for the skill.

RATE

If...	a student scores fewer than 85 wpm on this passage,
then...	identify reading rate difficulties (repetitions, ineffective or slow decoding). Help the student correctly read miscues and eliminate repetitions within a paragraph and then reread the paragraph several times. To provide additional practice, use one of the Fluency Routines, 11–14.

ACCURACY

If...	a student's Record of Oral Reading indicates problems decoding specific word types,
then...	analyze the types of miscues made. Have the student reread a sentence with a miscued word. If the student is unable to decode the miscued word, model and teach how to decode those word types. Then have the student read these types of words in books at the student's reading level.

RETELL Character, Setting, and Plot

If...	a student is unable to describe the characters, setting, or most important events in the plot,
then...	use the Character, Setting, and Plot graphic organizer (p. 120) or highlight words or phrases in the story to identify information about the characters, setting, or events. Then use Routine 15, Narrative Retelling, to model how to retell the important events in the plot.

COMPREHENSION Draw Conclusions

If...	a student is unable to draw conclusions in this story,
then...	explain that we draw a conclusion about things when we put new information together with what we already know. Use the Draw Conclusions graphic organizer (p. 124) to model how to use information from the story to draw a conclusion about Jim's feelings. Work with the student to draw other conclusions.

VOCABULARY Prefixes and Suffixes

If...	a student has trouble identifying prefixes and suffixes,
then...	explain to the student that the suffix *-hood* signifies "state or quality of" and the prefix *in-* means "not." Write the following words: *childhood, neighborhood, incorrect, inactive*. With the student, read each word, determine the meaning, and use it in a sentence.

WORD READING Prefixes *mis-, dis-, pre-, mid-*

If...	a student has difficulty correctly reading words with these prefixes,
then...	use Routine 4, Word Parts Strategy, to provide instruction and practice reading the words *midway, misbehave, disbelief, prejudge, discount, misunderstand, misread, preheat, preview, midnight, midday*.

Moving into Instruction 34

SUGGESTED SKILL INSTRUCTION If a student scores below 3 for a skill, use the recommendations below to provide additional instruction for the skill.

RATE

If...	a student scores fewer than 85 wpm on this passage,
then...	identify reading rate difficulties (repetitions, ineffective or slow decoding). Help the student correctly read miscues and eliminate repetitions within a paragraph and then reread the paragraph several times. To provide additional practice, use one of the Fluency Routines, 11–14.

ACCURACY

If...	a student's Record of Oral Reading indicates problems decoding specific word types,
then...	analyze the types of miscues made. Have the student reread a sentence with a miscued word. If the student is unable to decode the miscued word, model and teach how to decode those word types. Then have the student read these types of words in books at the student's reading level.

RETELL Character, Setting, and Plot

If...	a student is unable to describe the characters, setting, or most important events in the plot,
then...	use the Character, Setting, and Plot graphic organizer (p. 120) or highlight words or phrases in the story to identify information about the characters, setting, or events. Then use Routine 15, Narrative Retelling, to model how to retell the important events in the plot.

COMPREHENSION Draw Conclusions

If...	a student is unable to draw conclusions in this story,
then...	explain that we draw a conclusion about things when we put new information together with what we already know. Use the Draw Conclusions graphic organizer (p. 124) to model using information from the story to draw a conclusion about why Kate didn't want to race. Work with the student to draw other conclusions.

VOCABULARY Suffixes

If...	a student has trouble identifying suffixes,
then...	explain to the student that the suffix -*ist* means "one who practices" and -*ish* means "having the qualities of." Write the following words: *dentist, artist, selfish, bluish*. Ask the student to define each word and then use it in a sentence.

WORD READING Suffixes

If...	a student has difficulty correctly reading words with suffixes,
then...	use Routine 4, Word Parts Strategy, to provide instruction and practice reading the words *sandy, bluish, workers, bushy, watery, bookish, writer, teacher, selfish, creator*.

SUGGESTED SKILL INSTRUCTION If a student scores below 3 for a skill, use the recommendations below to provide additional instruction for the skill.

RATE

If...	a student scores fewer than 80 wpm on this passage,
then...	identify reading rate difficulties (repetitions, ineffective or slow decoding). Help the student correctly read miscues and eliminate repetitions within a paragraph and then reread the paragraph several times. To provide additional practice, use one of the Fluency Routines, 11–14.

ACCURACY

If...	a student's Record of Oral Reading indicates problems decoding specific word types,
then...	analyze the types of miscues made. Have the student reread a sentence with a miscued word. If the student is unable to decode the miscued word, model and teach how to decode those word types. Then have the student read these types of words in books at the student's reading level.

SUMMARIZE

If...	a student is unable to identify important ideas or details in this passage,
then...	model how to identify an important idea and the details that support it as you read aloud part of the passage. Then have the student do the same with the remainder of the passage. Use Routine 16, Summarizing, for additional instruction and practice.

COMPREHENSION Sequence

If...	a student is unable to identify sequence in this passage,
then...	read aloud the passage and model how to identify (circle or highlight) the first clue words/phrases that signal sequence *(first game)*. Have the student read aloud the rest of the passage and identify other clue words. Use the Sequence–Nonfiction graphic organizer (p. 119) to record the sequence of events.

VOCABULARY Context Clues

If...	a student has trouble identifying word meanings using context clues,
then...	point out specific words and phrases that provide clues to the unknown word *retired,* such as "...retired in 1976 after 23 seasons." Then help the student figure out the meaning of the word *valuable* by finding words or phrases that provide clues to its meaning.

WORD READING Syllable Patterns VC/V, V/CV

If...	a student has difficulty correctly reading words with these syllable patterns,
then...	use Routine 4, Word Parts Strategy, to provide instruction and practice reading the words *never, major, record, voted, retired, player, detail, music, lemon, tiger, legal, metal, pedal.*

Moving into Instruction **34**

SUGGESTED SKILL INSTRUCTION If a student scores below 3 for a skill, use the recommendations below to provide additional instruction for the skill.

RATE

If...	a student scores fewer than 80 wpm on this passage,
then...	identify reading rate difficulties (repetitions, ineffective or slow decoding). Help the student correctly read miscues and eliminate repetitions within a paragraph and then reread the paragraph several times. To provide additional practice, use one of the Fluency Routines, 11–14.

ACCURACY

If...	a student's Record of Oral Reading indicates problems decoding specific word types,
then...	analyze the types of miscues made. Have the student reread a sentence with a miscued word. If the student is unable to decode the miscued word, model and teach how to decode those word types. Then have the student read these types of words in books at the student's reading level.

SUMMARIZE

If...	a student is unable to identify important ideas or details in this passage,
then...	model how to identify an important idea and the details that support it as you read aloud part of the passage. Then have the student do the same with the remainder of the passage. Use Routine 16, Summarizing, for additional instruction and practice.

COMPREHENSION Sequence

If...	a student is unable to identify sequence in this passage,
then...	read aloud the passage and model how to identify (circle or highlight) the first clue words that signal sequence (first day). Have the student read aloud the rest of the passage and identify other clue words. Use the Sequence–Nonfiction graphic organizer (p. 119) to record the sequence of events.

VOCABULARY Antonyms

If...	a student has trouble identifying the meanings of antonyms,
then...	use the T-Chart graphic organizer (p. 125) and write *southern* in the left column. Ask the student to read the word and tell you what it means, and then have him or her say a word that has the opposite meaning. Have the student write the antonym in the right column of the chart. Repeat with other words: *first, healthy, good, biggest.*

WORD READING Common Syllables

If...	a student has difficulty correctly reading words with these common syllables,
then...	use Routine 4, Word Parts Strategy, to provide instruction and practice reading the words *celebration, features, mixture, conclusion, action, affection, mansion, picture, pasture, capture, culture.*

SUGGESTED SKILL INSTRUCTION If a student scores below 3 for a skill, use the recommendations below to provide additional instruction for the skill.

RATE

If...	a student scores fewer than 90 wpm on this passage,
then...	identify reading rate difficulties (repetitions, ineffective or slow decoding). Help the student correctly read miscues and eliminate repetitions within a paragraph and then reread the paragraph several times. To provide additional practice, use one of the Fluency Routines, 11–14.

ACCURACY

If...	a student's Record of Oral Reading indicates problems decoding specific word types,
then...	analyze the types of miscues made. Have the student reread a sentence with a miscued word. If the student is unable to decode the miscued word, model and teach how to decode those word types. Then have the student read these types of words in books at the student's reading level.

RETELL Character, Setting, and Plot

If...	a student is unable to describe the characters, setting, or most important events in the plot,
then...	use the Character, Setting, and Plot graphic organizer (p. 120) or highlight words or phrases in the story to identify information about the characters, setting, or events. Then use Routine 15, Narrative Retelling, to model how to retell the important events in the plot.

COMPREHENSION Compare and Contrast

If...	a student is unable to identify comparisons and contrasts in this selection,
then...	have the student read aloud the first paragraph. Help him or her to identify and record words and phrases that describe how the twin girls are alike and how they are different on a Venn Diagram graphic organizer (p. 122).

VOCABULARY Antonyms

If...	a student has trouble identifying the meanings of antonyms,
then...	use the T-Chart graphic organizer (p. 125) and write *different* in the left column. Ask the student to read the word and tell you what it means, and then ask the student to say a word that has the opposite meaning. Have the student write the antonym in the right column of the chart. Repeat with other words: *identical, dark, bright, real.*

WORD READING Multisyllabic Words

If...	a student has difficulty correctly reading multisyllabic words,
then...	use Routine 6, Multisyllabic Word Strategy, to provide instruction and practice reading the words *personalities, experiment, chattering, suddenly, library, noisily.*

Moving into Instruction 38

SUGGESTED SKILL INSTRUCTION If a student scores below 3 for a skill, use the recommendations below to provide additional instruction for the skill.

RATE

If...	a student scores fewer than 85 wpm on this passage,
then...	identify reading rate difficulties (repetitions, ineffective or slow decoding). Help the student correctly read miscues and eliminate repetitions within a paragraph and then reread the paragraph several times. To provide additional practice, use one of the Fluency Routines, 11–14.

ACCURACY

If...	a student's Record of Oral Reading indicates problems decoding specific word types,
then...	analyze the types of miscues made. Have the student reread a sentence with a miscued word. If the student is unable to decode the miscued word, model and teach how to decode those word types. Then have the student read these types of words in books at the student's reading level.

SUMMARIZE

If...	a student is unable to identify important ideas or details in this passage,
then...	model how to identify an important idea and the details that support it as you read aloud part of the passage. Then have the student do the same with the remainder of the passage. Use Routine 16, Summarizing, for additional instruction and practice.

COMPREHENSION Sequence

If...	a student is unable to identify sequence in this passage,
then...	read aloud the passage and model how to identify (circle or highlight) the first clue words/phrases that signal sequence (In 1876). Have the student read aloud the rest of the passage and identify other clue words. Use the Sequence–Nonfiction graphic organizer (p. 119) to record the sequence of events.

VOCABULARY Synonyms

If...	a student has trouble identifying synonyms,
then...	using the T-Chart graphic organizer (p. 125), write *independence* and *nations* in the left column. Ask the student to read each word and tell you what it means, and then have him or her say another word that has the same meaning. Write the synonyms in the right column of the chart. Repeat with other words: *build, idea, ships*.

WORD READING Multisyllabic Words

If...	a student has difficulty correctly reading multisyllabic words,
then...	use Routine 6, Multisyllabic Word Strategy, to provide instruction and practice reading the words *declaration, independence, celebrate, represents, liberty, together*.

Moving into Instruction 38

SUGGESTED SKILL INSTRUCTION If a student scores below 3 for a skill, use the recommendations below to provide additional instruction for the skill.

RATE

If...	a student scores fewer than 90 wpm on this passage,
then...	identify reading rate difficulties (repetitions, ineffective or slow decoding). Help the student correctly read miscues and eliminate repetitions within a paragraph and then reread the paragraph several times. To provide additional practice, use one of the Fluency Routines, 11–14.

ACCURACY

If...	a student's Record of Oral Reading indicates problems decoding specific word types,
then...	analyze the types of miscues made. Have the student reread a sentence with a miscued word. If the student is unable to decode the miscued word, model and teach how to decode those word types. Then have the student read these types of words in books at the student's reading level.

RETELL Character, Setting, and Plot

If...	a student is unable to describe the characters, setting, or most important events in the plot,
then...	use the Character, Setting, and Plot graphic organizer (p. 120) or highlight words or phrases in the story to identify information about the characters, setting, or events. Then use Routine 15, Narrative Retelling, to model how to retell the important events in the plot.

COMPREHENSION Cause and Effect

If...	a student is unable to identify cause and effect in the text,
then...	use the Cause and Effect graphic organizer (p. 123) to model how to find out why Marco's ankle is swollen. Then have the student find why someone tells Marco "Nice writing" at the end. Remind the student that a cause-and-effect relationship consists of what happened and why.

VOCABULARY Multiple-Meaning Words

If...	a student cannot identify the correct meanings for the multiple-meaning words in the selection,
then...	model using different definitions of the word *lead* (to show the way; be ahead in a contest) in context. Discuss which definition makes the most sense in this passage. Help the student use this method to determine the correct meanings of the words *seconds, row,* and *back*.

WORD READING Common Syllables *-tive, -sive, -ity*

If...	a student has difficulty correctly reading words with common syllables *-tive, -sive, -ity,*
then...	use Routine 4, Word Parts Strategy, to provide instruction and practice reading the words *positive, massive, electricity, active, cursive, motive, narrative, passive, aggressive, cavity, gravity*.

Moving into Instruction **38**

SUGGESTED SKILL INSTRUCTION If a student scores below 3 for a skill, use the recommendations below to provide additional instruction for the skill.

RATE

If...	a student scores fewer than 85 wpm on this passage,
then...	identify reading rate difficulties (repetitions, ineffective or slow decoding). Help the student correctly read miscues and eliminate repetitions within a paragraph and then reread the paragraph several times. To provide additional practice, use one of the Fluency Routines, 11–14.

ACCURACY

If...	a student's Record of Oral Reading indicates problems decoding specific word types,
then...	analyze the types of miscues made. Have the student reread a sentence with a miscued word. If the student is unable to decode the miscued word, model and teach how to decode those word types. Then have the student read these types of words in books at the student's reading level.

SUMMARIZE

If...	a student is unable to identify important ideas or details in this passage,
then...	model how to identify an important idea and the details that support it as you read aloud part of the passage. Then have the student do the same with the remainder of the passage. Use Routine 16, Summarizing, for additional instruction and practice.

COMPREHENSION Cause and Effect

If...	a student is unable to identify cause and effect in the text,
then...	use the Cause and Effect graphic organizer (p. 123) to model how to find what happens when a vibration contacts the air. Then have the student find what happens when a sound wave contacts our ears. Remind the student that a cause-and-effect relationship consists of what happened and why.

VOCABULARY Suffixes

If...	a student has trouble identifying suffixes,
then...	explain to the student what the suffixes -er (one who) and -ion (action or state of) signify. Write the following words: *vibration, attention, teacher, painter*. With the student, read each word, determine the meaning, and use it in a sentence.

WORD READING Suffixes -able, -ible, -hood, -ment

If...	a student has difficulty correctly reading words with these suffixes,
then...	use Routine 4, Word Parts Strategy, to provide instruction and practice reading the words *understandable, terrible, childhood, instrument, readable, visible, adulthood, boyhood, payment, improvement*.

Moving into Instruction **38**

SUGGESTED SKILL INSTRUCTION If a student scores below 3 for a skill, use the recommendations below to provide additional instruction for the skill.

RATE

If...	a student scores fewer than 85 wpm on this passage,
then...	identify reading rate difficulties (repetitions, ineffective or slow decoding). Help the student correctly read miscues and eliminate repetitions within a paragraph and then reread the paragraph several times. To provide additional practice, use one of the Fluency Routines, 11–14.

ACCURACY

If...	a student's Record of Oral Reading indicates problems decoding specific word types,
then...	analyze the types of miscues made. Have the student reread a sentence with a miscued word. If the student is unable to decode the miscued word, model and teach how to decode those word types. Then have the student read these types of words in books at the student's reading level.

SUMMARIZE

If...	a student is unable to identify important ideas or details in this passage,
then...	model how to identify an important idea and the details that support it as you read aloud part of the passage. Then have the student do the same with the remainder of the passage. Use Routine 16, Summarizing, for additional instruction and practice.

COMPREHENSION Compare and Contrast

If...	a student is unable to identify comparisons and contrasts in this selection,
then...	have the student read aloud the first three paragraphs. Together identify the two sources of energy. Record how these energy sources are alike and different on a Venn Diagram graphic organizer (p. 122).

VOCABULARY Context Clues

If...	a student has trouble identifying word meanings using context clues,
then...	point out specific words and phrases that provide clues to the unknown word *solar*, such as "Energy from the sun, or solar power." Then help the student determine the meaning of the word *nonrenewable* by finding words or phrases that provide clues to its meaning.

WORD READING Syllable Patterns VCCCV and V/V

If...	a student has difficulty correctly reading words with these syllable patterns,
then...	use Routine 4, Word Parts Strategy, to provide instruction and practice reading the words *radio, create, hundreds, conflict, contract, extra, improve, instead, react, biology, audio, area, media.*

Moving into Instruction **38**

SUGGESTED SKILL INSTRUCTION If a student scores below 3 for a skill, use the recommendations below to provide additional instruction for the skill.

RATE

If...	a student scores fewer than 100 wpm on this passage,
then...	identify reading rate difficulties (repetitions, ineffective or slow decoding). Help the student correctly read miscues and eliminate repetitions within a paragraph and then reread the paragraph several times. To provide additional practice, use one of the Fluency Routines, 11–14.

ACCURACY

If...	a student's Record of Oral Reading indicates problems decoding specific word types,
then...	analyze the types of miscues made. Have the student reread a sentence with a miscued word. If the student is unable to decode the miscued word, model and teach how to decode those word types. Then have the student read these types of words in continuous texts.

SUMMARIZE

If...	a student is unable to identify important ideas or details in this passage,
then...	model how to identify an important idea and the details that support it as you begin to read aloud part of the passage. Then have the student do the same with the remainder of the passage. Use Routine 16, Summarizing, for additional instruction and practice.

COMPREHENSION Draw Conclusions

If...	a student is unable to draw conclusions in this selection,
then...	reread the passage together. Then use the Draw Conclusions graphic organizer (p. 124) to model how to use information from the passage to draw a conclusion about fossils or dinosaurs. Work with the student to draw other conclusions.

VOCABULARY Multiple-Meaning Words

If...	a student cannot identify the appropriate meanings of multiple-meaning words in the selection,
then...	model using different definitions of the word *plants* (living things; building used in manufacturing) in context and discuss which definition makes the most sense in the passage. Then help the student use this method to determine the correct meanings of the words *remains, way, rock,* and *ground*.

WORD READING Less Common Vowel Patterns *augh, ough, eigh*

If...	a student has difficulty correctly reading words with these vowel patterns,
then...	use Routine 2, Whole-Word Blending, to provide instruction and practice reading the words *caught, through, weighed, laugh, taught, bought, enough, sleigh, height, eight*.

SUGGESTED SKILL INSTRUCTION If a student scores below 3 for a skill, use the recommendations below to provide additional instruction for the skill.

RATE	
If...	a student scores fewer than 105 wpm on this passage,
then...	identify reading rate difficulties (repetitions, ineffective or slow decoding). Help the student correctly read miscues and eliminate repetitions within a paragraph and then reread the paragraph several times. To provide additional practice, use one of the Fluency Routines, 11–14.

ACCURACY	
If...	a student's Record of Oral Reading indicates problems decoding specific word types,
then...	analyze the types of miscues made. Have the student reread a sentence with a miscued word. If the student is unable to decode the miscued word, model and teach how to decode those word types. Then have the student read these types of words in continuous texts.

RETELL Character, Setting, and Plot	
If...	a student is unable to describe the characters, setting, or most important events in the plot,
then...	use the Character, Setting, and Plot graphic organizer (p. 120) or highlight words or phrases in the story to identify information about the characters, setting, or events. Then use Routine 15, Narrative Retelling, to model how to retell the important events in the plot.

COMPREHENSION Cause and Effect	
If...	a student is unable to identify cause and effect in the text,
then...	use the Cause and Effect graphic organizer (p. 123) to model how to find out why Sam's parents take him to a game. Record it on the chart. Then, together with the student, record why the day is a dream come true for Sam. Remind the student that a cause-and-effect relationship consists of what happened and why.

VOCABULARY Roots *bio, photo*	
If...	a student has trouble identifying the meanings of the words *photographs* and *biographies*,
then...	explain to the student what the roots *bio* (life) and *photo* (light) mean. Work with the student to give a meaning for each of these words and use each in a sentence: *biography, biology, photograph, photocopy*.

WORD READING Two-Syllable Base Words with Endings	
If...	a student has difficulty correctly reading two-syllable base words with endings,
then...	use Routine 4, Word Parts Strategy, to provide instruction and practice reading the words *happiest, dribbling, excited, finally, beginning, bubbling, nervously, questioning, answering, explaining*.

Moving into Instruction **40**

SUGGESTED SKILL INSTRUCTION If a student scores below 3 for a skill, use the recommendations below to provide additional instruction for the skill.

RATE

If...	a student scores fewer than 100 wpm on this passage,
then...	identify reading rate difficulties (repetitions, ineffective or slow decoding). Help the student correctly read miscues and eliminate repetitions within a paragraph and then reread the paragraph several times. To provide additional practice, use one of the Fluency Routines, 11–14.

ACCURACY

If...	a student's Record of Oral Reading indicates problems decoding specific word types,
then...	analyze the types of miscues made. Have the student reread a sentence with a miscued word. If the student is unable to decode the miscued word, model and teach how to decode those word types. Then have the student read these types of words in continuous texts.

SUMMARIZE

If...	a student is unable to identify important ideas or details in this passage,
then...	model how to identify an important idea and the details that support it as you read aloud part of the passage. Then have the student do the same with the remainder of the passage. Use Routine 16, Summarizing, for additional instruction and practice.

COMPREHENSION Sequence

If...	a student is unable to identify sequence in this selection,
then...	use a Sequence–Nonfiction graphic organizer (p. 119) to model how to identify signal words for sequence in the text. Then have the student identify sequence words such as *first, then, next,* and *today* to help the student complete the graphic organizer.

VOCABULARY Prefixes and Suffixes *im-, -tion*

If...	a student has trouble determining the meanings of words with prefixes and suffixes,
then...	explain to the student that the prefix *im-* means "not" and that the suffix *-tion* signifies "action" or "state of." Write the following words: *impossible, information, impatient, celebration, capitalization.* With the student, read each word, determine the meaning, and use each word in a sentence.

WORD READING Syllable Patterns VC/CV, C + *le*, V/CV and VC/V

If...	a student has difficulty correctly reading words with these syllable patterns,
then...	use Routine 4, Word Parts Strategy, to provide instruction and practice reading the words *pictures, possible, robots, Spirit, bacon, scenic, taken, panic, rebel, people, capable, handle, expel.*

Moving into Instruction **40**

SUGGESTED SKILL INSTRUCTION If a student scores below 3 for a skill, use the recommendations below to provide additional instruction for the skill.

RATE

If...	a student scores fewer than 105 wpm on this passage,
then...	identify reading rate difficulties (repetitions, ineffective or slow decoding). Help the student correctly read miscues and eliminate repetitions within a paragraph and then reread the paragraph several times. To provide additional practice, use one of the Fluency Routines, 11–14.

ACCURACY

If...	a student's Record of Oral Reading indicates problems decoding specific word types,
then...	analyze the types of miscues made. Have the student reread a sentence with a miscued word. If the student is unable to decode the miscued word, model and teach how to decode those word types. Then have the student read these types of words in continuous texts.

RETELL Character, Setting, and Plot

If...	a student is unable to describe the characters, setting, or most important events in the plot,
then...	use the Character, Setting, and Plot graphic organizer (p. 120) or highlight words or phrases in the story to identify information about the characters, setting, or events. Then use Routine 15, Narrative Retelling, to model how to retell the important events in the plot.

COMPREHENSION Compare and Contrast

If...	a student is unable to identify comparisons and contrasts in this selection,
then...	explain that when we compare and contrast two things, we tell how they are alike and how they are different. Have the student read aloud the fourth through sixth paragraphs. Together record how stars and the planet Mars are alike and different on a Venn Diagram graphic organizer (p. 122).

VOCABULARY Context Clues

If...	a student has trouble identifying word meanings using context clues,
then...	point out specific words and phrases that provide clues to the meaning of the word *twinkle*, such as "...stars appear to twinkle. Stars wink on and off." Then help the student figure out the meanings of *stationary* and *anxious* by finding words or phrases that provide clues to their meanings.

WORD READING Irregular Spellings

If...	a student has difficulty correctly reading words with irregular spellings,
then...	use Routine 8, Nondecodable Words Strategy, to provide instruction and practice reading the words *cousin, mountains, cushion, stationary, anxious, answer, machine, ocean, said, should, again*.

SUGGESTED SKILL INSTRUCTION If a student scores below 3 for a skill, use the recommendations below to provide additional instruction for the skill.

RATE

If...	a student scores fewer than 100 wpm on this passage,
then...	identify reading rate difficulties (repetitions, ineffective or slow decoding). Help the student correctly read miscues and eliminate repetitions within a paragraph and then reread the paragraph several times. To provide additional practice, use one of the Fluency Routines, 11–14.

ACCURACY

If...	a student's Record of Oral Reading indicates problems decoding specific word types,
then...	analyze the types of miscues made. Have the student reread a sentence with a miscued word. If the student is unable to decode the miscued word, model and teach how to decode those word types. Then have the student read these types of words in continuous texts.

SUMMARIZE

If...	a student is unable to identify important ideas or details in this passage,
then...	model how to identify an important idea and the details that support it as you read aloud part of the passage. Then have the student do the same with the remainder of the passage. Use Routine 16, Summarizing, for additional instruction and practice.

COMPREHENSION Sequence

If...	a student is unable to identify sequence in this selection,
then...	write four events from the passage that take place in the food chain on index cards, along with the words or phrases that indicate their sequence. Have the student arrange the cards in sequence, reminding the student to pay close attention to sequence words.

VOCABULARY Context Clues

If...	a student has trouble identifying word meanings using context clues,
then...	point out specific words and phrases that provide clues to the meaning of the word *consume*, such as "...from the food that you consume." Then help the student figure out the meanings of *absorb* and *consume* by finding words or phrases that provide clues to their meanings.

WORD READING Multisyllabic Words

If...	a student has difficulty correctly reading multisyllabic words,
then...	use Routine 6, Multisyllabic Word Strategy, to provide instruction and practice reading the words *majority* and *energy*.

Moving into Instruction 40

SUGGESTED SKILL INSTRUCTION If a student scores below 3 for a skill, use the recommendations below to provide additional instruction for the skill.

RATE

If...	a student scores fewer than 105 wpm on this passage,
then...	identify reading rate difficulties (repetitions, ineffective or slow decoding). Help the student correctly read miscues and eliminate repetitions within a paragraph and then reread the paragraph several times. To provide additional practice, use one of the Fluency Routines, 11–14.

ACCURACY

If...	a student's Record of Oral Reading indicates problems decoding specific word types,
then...	analyze the types of miscues made. Have the student reread a sentence with a miscued word. If the student is unable to decode the miscued word, model and teach how to decode those word types. Then have the student read these types of words in continuous texts.

RETELL Character, Setting, and Plot

If...	a student is unable to describe the characters, setting, or most important events in the plot,
then...	use the Character, Setting, and Plot graphic organizer (p. 120) or highlight words or phrases in the story to identify information about the characters, setting, or events. Then use Routine 15, Narrative Retelling, to model how to retell the important events in the plot.

COMPREHENSION Draw Conclusions

If...	a student is unable to draw conclusions in this selection,
then...	reread the passage together. Then use the Draw Conclusions graphic organizer (p. 124) to model how to use information from the passage to draw a conclusion about the newest invention. Work with the student to draw other conclusions.

VOCABULARY Context Clues

If...	a student has trouble identifying word meanings using context clues,
then...	point out specific words and phrases that provide clues to the meaning of the word *transcribed*, such as "transcribed words into secret letters." Then help the student figure out the meaning of *platform* by finding words or phrases that provide clues to its meaning.

WORD READING Common Syllables

If...	a student has difficulty correctly reading words with common syllables,
then...	use Routine 4, Word Parts Strategy, to provide instruction and practice reading the words *invention, confusion, pleasure, structure, capture, injure, nature, secure, vulture, situation, question, option.*

Moving into Instruction **40**

SUGGESTED SKILL INSTRUCTION If a student scores below 3 for a skill, use the recommendations below to provide additional instruction for the skill.

RATE

If...	a student scores fewer than 100 wpm on this passage,
then...	identify reading rate difficulties (repetitions, ineffective or slow decoding). Help the student correctly read miscues and eliminate repetitions within a paragraph and then reread the paragraph several times. To provide additional practice, use one of the Fluency Routines, 11–14.

ACCURACY

If...	a student's Record of Oral Reading indicates problems decoding specific word types,
then...	analyze the types of miscues made. Have the student reread a sentence with a miscued word. If the student is unable to decode the miscued word, model and teach how to decode those word types. Then have the student read these types of words in continuous texts.

SUMMARIZE

If...	a student is unable to identify important ideas or details in this passage,
then...	model how to identify an important idea and the details that support it as you read aloud part of the passage. Then have the student do the same with the remainder of the passage. Use Routine 16, Summarizing, for additional instruction and practice.

COMPREHENSION Draw Conclusions

If...	a student is unable to draw conclusions in this selection,
then...	reread the passage together. Then use the Draw Conclusions graphic organizer (p. 124) to model how to use information from the passage to draw a conclusion about roadrunners. Work with the student to draw other conclusions.

VOCABULARY Suffix *-ly*

If...	a student has trouble identifying suffixes,
then...	explain to the student that the suffix *-ly* means "having the characteristics of." Write the following words: *mostly, briefly, amazingly, believably*. With the student, read each word, determine the meaning, and use it in a sentence.

WORD READING Vowel Patterns *ey, ie, ei*

If...	a student has difficulty correctly reading words with these vowel patterns,
then...	use Routine 2, Whole-Word Blending, to provide instruction and practice reading the words *preys, seize, briefly, piece, field, alley, donkey, greyhound, geyser, height, weight, vein.*

Moving into Instruction 40

SUGGESTED SKILL INSTRUCTION If a student scores below 3 for a skill, use the recommendations below to provide additional instruction for the skill.

RATE

If...	a student scores fewer than 105 wpm on this passage,
then...	identify reading rate difficulties (repetitions, ineffective or slow decoding). Help the student correctly read miscues and eliminate repetitions within a paragraph and then reread the paragraph several times. To provide additional practice, use one of the Fluency Routines, 11–14.

ACCURACY

If...	a student's Record of Oral Reading indicates problems decoding specific word types,
then...	analyze the types of miscues made. Have the student reread a sentence with a miscued word. If the student is unable to decode the miscued word, model and teach how to decode those word types. Then have the student read these types of words in continuous texts.

RETELL Character, Setting, and Plot

If...	a student is unable to describe the characters, setting, or most important events in the plot,
then...	use the Character, Setting, and Plot graphic organizer (p. 120) or highlight words or phrases in the story to identify information about the characters, setting, or events. Then use Routine 15, Narrative Retelling, to model how to retell the important events in the plot.

COMPREHENSION Cause and Effect

If...	a student is unable to identify cause and effect in the text,
then...	use the Cause and Effect graphic organizer (p. 123) to model how to find out what causes Riz to hop so fast. Record it on the chart. Then, together with the student, record how most of the robots are affected by going underwater. Remind the student that a cause-and-effect relationship consists of what happened and why.

VOCABULARY Context Clues

If...	a student has trouble identifying word meanings using context clues,
then...	point out specific words and phrases that provide clues to the meaning of the word *triathlon*, such as "The race...had three parts." Then help the student figure out the meanings of *biannual* and *springs* by finding words or phrases that provide clues to their meanings.

WORD READING Prefixes *bi-, tri-, sub-*

If...	a student has difficulty correctly reading words with these prefixes,
then...	use Routine 4, Word Parts Strategy, to provide instruction and practice reading the words *biannual, bicycle, tricycle, submarine, bicentennial, triangle, sublevel, submarine*.

Moving into Instruction 40

SUGGESTED SKILL INSTRUCTION If a student scores below 3 for a skill, use the recommendations below to provide additional instruction for the skill.

RATE

If...	a student scores fewer than 100 wpm on this passage,
then...	identify reading rate difficulties (repetitions, ineffective or slow decoding). Help the student correctly read miscues and eliminate repetitions within a paragraph and then reread the paragraph several times. To provide additional practice, use one of the Fluency Routines, 11–14.

ACCURACY

If...	a student's Record of Oral Reading indicates problems decoding specific word types,
then...	analyze the types of miscues made. Have the student reread a sentence with a miscued word. If the student is unable to decode the miscued word, model and teach how to decode those word types. Then have the student read these types of words in continuous texts.

SUMMARIZE

If...	a student is unable to identify important ideas or details in this passage,
then...	model how to identify an important idea and the details that support it as you read aloud part of the passage. Then have the student do the same with the remainder of the passage. Use Routine 16, Summarizing, for additional instruction and practice.

COMPREHENSION Sequence

If...	a student is unable to identify sequence of events in this selection,
then...	use a Sequence–Nonfiction graphic organizer (p. 119) to model how to identify a signal word or date for sequence in the text. Then have the student identify other sequence words, such as *early 1800s; May 14, 1804; July; winter;* and *spring.*

VOCABULARY Multiple-Meaning Words

If...	a student cannot identify the appropriate meanings of multiple-meaning words in the selection,
then...	model using different definitions of the word *trip* (to stumble or slip; a journey) in context and discuss which definition makes the most sense in the passage. Then help the student use this method to determine the correct meanings of the words *spring, part, spending,* and *plants.*

WORD READING Suffixes *-en, -y, -or, -ist*

If...	a student has difficulty correctly reading words with these suffixes,
then...	use Routine 4, Word Parts Strategy, to provide instruction and practice reading the words *chosen, chilly, collector, artist, broaden, fallen, jumpy, smelly, educator, warrior, artist, guitarist.*

Moving into Instruction 40

SUGGESTED SKILL INSTRUCTION If a student scores below 3 for a skill, use the recommendations below to provide additional instruction for the skill.

RATE

If...	a student scores fewer than 105 wpm on this passage,
then...	identify reading rate difficulties (repetitions, ineffective or slow decoding). Help the student correctly read miscues and eliminate repetitions within a paragraph and then reread the paragraph several times. To provide additional practice, use one of the Fluency Routines, 11–14.

ACCURACY

If...	a student's Record of Oral Reading indicates problems decoding specific word types,
then...	analyze the types of miscues made. Have the student reread a sentence with a miscued word. If the student is unable to decode the miscued word, model and teach how to decode those word types. Then have the student read these types of words in continuous texts.

RETELL Character, Setting, and Plot

If...	a student is unable to describe the characters, setting, or most important events in the plot,
then...	use the Character, Setting, and Plot graphic organizer (p. 120) or highlight words or phrases in the story to identify information about the characters, setting, or events. Then use Routine 15, Narrative Retelling, to model how to retell the important events in the plot.

COMPREHENSION Compare and Contrast

If...	a student is unable to identify comparisons and contrasts in this selection,
then...	model how to circle words or phrases that tell the reader about the two girls in the story and what they are like, based on what they say and do. Then have the student complete a Venn Diagram graphic organizer (p. 122) to chart how the girls in the story are similar and different.

VOCABULARY Roots *tele, photo*

If...	a student has trouble identifying the meanings of the words *photocopies* and *telephone*,
then...	explain to the student what the roots *tele* (far) and *photo* (light) mean. Work with the student to give a meaning for each of these words and use each in a sentence: *telegraph, telescope, photograph, telephoto.*

WORD READING Greek Roots *tele, phon, photo*

If...	a student has difficulty correctly reading words with these Greek roots,
then...	use Routine 6, Multisyllabic Word Strategy, to provide instruction and practice reading the words *photocopies, phones, photograph, telephone, telegraph, microphone, headphones, symphony, telecast.*

Moving into Instruction 40

SUGGESTED SKILL INSTRUCTION If a student scores below 3 for a skill, use the recommendations below to provide additional instruction for the skill.

RATE

If...	a student scores fewer than 100 wpm on this passage,
then...	identify reading rate difficulties (repetitions, ineffective or slow decoding). Help the student correctly read miscues and eliminate repetitions within a paragraph and then reread the paragraph several times. To provide additional practice, use one of the Fluency Routines, 11–14.

ACCURACY

If...	a student's Record of Oral Reading indicates problems decoding specific word types,
then...	analyze the types of miscues made. Have the student reread a sentence with a miscued word. If the student is unable to decode the miscued word, model and teach how to decode those word types. Then have the student read these types of words in continuous texts.

SUMMARIZE

If...	a student is unable to identify important ideas or details in this passage,
then...	model how to identify an important idea and the details that support it as you read aloud part of the passage. Then have the student do the same with the remainder of the passage. Use Routine 16, Summarizing, for additional instruction and practice.

COMPREHENSION Cause and Effect

If...	a student is unable to identify cause and effect in the text,
then...	use the Cause and Effect graphic organizer (p. 123) to model how to find out what happened when women became active in the voting rights movement. Record it on the chart. Then have the student use the same method to find what happened to women during WWI. Have the student record it on the chart.

VOCABULARY Multiple-Meaning Words

If...	a student cannot identify the appropriate meanings of multiple-meaning words in the selection,
then...	model using different definitions of the word *right* (correct; the opposite of the direction left; something that is properly given to someone) in context and discuss which definition makes sense in the passage. Then help the student determine the correct meaning of the word *state*.

WORD READING Common Syllables *-ify, -sive, -ity*

If...	a student has difficulty correctly reading words with these common syllables,
then...	use Routine 6, Multisyllabic Word Strategy, to provide instruction and practice reading the words *intensify, persuasive, opportunity, defensive, explosive, justify, classify, activity, curiosity.*

Moving into Instruction 40

SUGGESTED SKILL INSTRUCTION If a student scores below 3 for a skill, use the recommendations below to provide additional instruction for the skill.

RATE

If...	a student scores fewer than 105 wpm on this passage,
then...	identify reading rate difficulties (repetitions, ineffective or slow decoding). Help the student correctly read miscues and eliminate repetitions within a paragraph and then reread the paragraph several times. To provide additional practice, use one of the Fluency Routines, 11–14.

ACCURACY

If...	a student's Record of Oral Reading indicates problems decoding specific word types,
then...	analyze the types of miscues made. Have the student reread a sentence with a miscued word. If the student is unable to decode the miscued word, model and teach how to decode those word types. Then have the student read these types of words in continuous texts.

RETELL Character, Setting, and Plot

If...	a student is unable to describe the characters, setting, or most important events in the plot,
then...	use the Character, Setting, and Plot graphic organizer (p. 120) or highlight words or phrases in the story to identify information about the characters, setting, or events. Then use Routine 15, Narrative Retelling, to model how to retell the important events in the plot.

COMPREHENSION Draw Conclusions

If...	a student is unable to draw conclusions in this selection,
then...	reread the passage together. Then use the Draw Conclusions graphic organizer (p. 124) to model using information from the passage to draw a conclusion about Aiden's idea. Work with the student to draw other conclusions.

VOCABULARY Roots *audi, micro*

If...	a student has trouble identifying the meanings of the words *auditorium* and *microphone*,
then...	explain to the student what the roots *audi* (to hear) and *micro* (small) mean. Work with the student to give a meaning for each of these words and use each in a sentence: *audiobook, microscope.*

WORD READING Latin Roots *audi, port, uni*

If...	a student has difficulty correctly reading words with these Latin roots,
then...	use Routine 6, Multisyllabic Word Strategy, to provide instruction and practice reading the words *auditorium, reported, transport, uniforms, audition, airport, export, import, universe, unicorn.*

Moving into Instruction 40

SUGGESTED SKILL INSTRUCTION If a student scores below 3 for a skill, use the recommendations below to provide additional instruction for the skill.

RATE

If...	a student scores fewer than 100 wpm on this passage,
then...	identify reading rate difficulties (repetitions, ineffective or slow decoding). Help the student correctly read miscues and eliminate repetitions within a paragraph and then reread the paragraph several times. To provide additional practice, use one of the Fluency Routines, 11–14.

ACCURACY

If...	a student's Record of Oral Reading indicates problems decoding specific word types,
then...	analyze the types of miscues made. Have the student reread a sentence with a miscued word. If the student is unable to decode the miscued word, model and teach how to decode those word types. Then have the student read these types of words in continuous texts.

SUMMARIZE

If...	a student is unable to identify important ideas or details in this passage,
then...	model how to identify an important idea and the details that support it as you read aloud part of the passage. Then have the student do the same with the remainder of the passage. Use Routine 16, Summarizing, for additional instruction and practice.

COMPREHENSION Compare and Contrast

If...	a student is unable to identify comparisons and contrasts in this selection,
then...	model how to locate and then underline in the passage an aspect of travel to California in 1848 versus today. Help the student use different colors to underline additional aspects. Then have the student complete a T-Chart graphic organizer (p. 125) to chart how travel then and now are alike and different.

VOCABULARY Prefixes and Suffixes *in-, -or*

If...	a student has trouble identifying prefixes and suffixes,
then...	explain to the student that the prefix *in-* means "not" and that the suffix *-or* signifies "someone who." Write the following words: *informal, infrequent, prospectors, director.* With the student, read each word, determine the meaning, and use it in a sentence.

WORD READING Prefixes *im-, in-, non-*

If...	a student has difficulty correctly reading words with these prefixes,
then...	use Routine 4, Word Parts Strategy, to provide instruction and practice reading the words *impossible, indirect, nontraditional, imbalance, improper, incorrect, inactive, incapable, nondairy, nonliving.*

Moving into Instruction 40

SUGGESTED SKILL INSTRUCTION If a student scores below 3 for a skill, use the recommendations below to provide additional instruction for the skill.

RATE

If…	a student scores fewer than 105 wpm on this passage,
then…	identify reading rate difficulties (repetitions, ineffective or slow decoding). Help the student correctly read miscues and eliminate repetitions within a paragraph and then reread the paragraph several times. To provide additional practice, use one of the Fluency Routines, 11–14.

ACCURACY

If…	a student's Record of Oral Reading indicates problems decoding specific word types,
then…	analyze the types of miscues made. Have the student reread a sentence with a miscued word. If the student is unable to decode the miscued word, model and teach how to decode those word types. Then have the student read these types of words in continuous texts.

RETELL Character, Setting, and Plot

If…	a student is unable to describe the characters, setting, or most important events in the plot,
then…	use the Character, Setting, and Plot graphic organizer (p. 120) or highlight words or phrases in the story to identify information about the characters, setting, or events. Then use Routine 15, Narrative Retelling, to model how to retell the important events in the plot.

COMPREHENSION Sequence

If…	a student is unable to identify sequence in this selection,
then…	write four events from the passage that have to do with Jake's class field trip on index cards, along with the words or phrases that indicate their sequence. Have the student arrange the cards in sequence, reminding the student to pay close attention to sequence words.

VOCABULARY Context Clues

If…	a student has trouble identifying word meanings using context clues,
then…	point out specific words and phrases that provide clues to the meaning of the word *armor*, such as "…two knights wearing glistening armor." Then help the student figure out the meaning of *residents* by finding words or phrases that provide clues to its meaning.

WORD READING Suffixes *-hood, -ment, -ant, -ent*

If…	a student has difficulty correctly reading words with these suffixes,
then…	use Routine 4, Word Parts Strategy, to provide instruction and practice reading the words *knighthood, excitement, hesitant, residents, childhood, refreshment, extravagant, observant, consistent.*

Moving into Instruction **40**

SUGGESTED SKILL INSTRUCTION If a student scores below 3 for a skill, use the recommendations below to provide additional instruction for the skill.

RATE

If...	a student scores fewer than 100 wpm on this passage,
then...	identify reading rate difficulties (repetitions, ineffective or slow decoding). Help the student correctly read miscues and eliminate repetitions within a paragraph and then reread the paragraph several times. To provide additional practice, use one of the Fluency Routines, 11–14.

ACCURACY

If...	a student's Record of Oral Reading indicates problems decoding specific word types,
then...	analyze the types of miscues made. Have the student reread a sentence with a miscued word. If the student is unable to decode the miscued word, model and teach how to decode those word types. Then have the student read these types of words in continuous texts.

SUMMARIZE

If...	a student is unable to identify important ideas or details in this passage,
then...	model how to identify an important idea and the details that support it as you read aloud part of the passage. Then have the student do the same with the remainder of the passage. Use Routine 16, Summarizing, for additional instruction and practice.

COMPREHENSION Sequence

If...	a student is unable to identify sequence in this selection,
then...	model how to circle signal words for sequence in the text, such as *1941*. Remind the student that dates can provide clues to sequence. Then have the student circle the rest of the signal words and complete a Sequence–Nonfiction graphic organizer (p. 119).

VOCABULARY Context Clues

If...	a student has trouble identifying word meanings using context clues,
then...	point out specific words and phrases that provide clues to the meaning of the word *military*, such as "…entered the war; American soldiers…" Then help the student figure out the meanings of *cooperated* and *Navajo* by finding words or phrases that provide clues to their meanings.

WORD READING Syllable Patterns VCCCV, VV

If...	a student has difficulty correctly reading words with these syllable patterns,
then...	use Routine 2, Whole-Word Blending, to provide instruction and practice reading the words *understand, idea, cooperated, battle, stereo, reliable, material, diamond, subtract, sandwich, pumpkin.*

SUGGESTED SKILL INSTRUCTION If a student scores below 3 for a skill, use the recommendations below to provide additional instruction for the skill.

RATE

If...	a student scores fewer than 115 wpm on this passage,
then...	identify reading rate difficulties (repetitions, ineffective or slow decoding). Help the student correctly read miscues and eliminate repetitions within a paragraph and then reread the paragraph several times. To provide additional practice, use one of the Fluency Routines, 11–14.

ACCURACY

If...	a student's Record of Oral Reading indicates problems decoding specific word types,
then...	analyze the types of miscues made. Have the student reread a sentence with a miscued word. If the student is unable to decode the miscued word, model and teach how to decode those word types. Then have the student read these types of words in continuous texts.

RETELL Character, Setting, and Plot

If...	a student is unable to describe the characters, setting, or most important events in the plot,
then...	use the Character, Setting, and Plot graphic organizer (p. 120) or highlight words or phrases in the story to identify information about the characters, setting, or events. Then use Routine 15, Narrative Retelling, to model how to retell the important events in the plot.

COMPREHENSION Compare and Contrast

If...	a student is unable to identify comparisons and contrasts in this selection,
then...	reread the passage with the student and discuss what is being compared and contrasted. Then work with the student to complete a Venn Diagram graphic organizer (p. 122) or T-Chart (p. 125) to list similarities and differences between the earthquake and the hurricane.

VOCABULARY Context Clues

If...	a student has trouble identifying word meanings using context clues,
then...	point out specific words and phrases that provide clues to the meaning of the word *warn*, such as "...so we had time to board up the windows..." Then help the student figure out the meanings of *damage* and *overpass* by finding words or phrases that provide clues to their meanings.

WORD READING Multisyllabic Words

If...	a student has difficulty correctly reading multisyllabic words,
then...	use Routine 6, Multisyllabic Word Strategy, for instruction and practice reading the words *befriended, hurricane, expensive, gigantic*.

Moving into Instruction **50**

SUGGESTED SKILL INSTRUCTION If a student scores below 3 for a skill, use the recommendations below to provide additional instruction for the skill.

RATE

If...	a student scores fewer than 115 wpm on this passage,
then...	identify reading rate difficulties (repetitions, ineffective or slow decoding). Help the student correctly read miscues and eliminate repetitions within a paragraph and then reread the paragraph several times. To provide additional practice, use one of the Fluency Routines, 11–14.

ACCURACY

If...	a student's Record of Oral Reading indicates problems decoding specific word types,
then...	analyze the types of miscues made. Have the student reread a sentence with a miscued word. If the student is unable to decode the miscued word, model and teach how to decode those word types. Then have the student read these types of words in continuous texts.

RETELL Character, Setting, and Plot

If...	a student is unable to describe the characters, setting, or most important events in the plot,
then...	use the Character, Setting, and Plot graphic organizer (p. 120) or highlight words or phrases in the story to identify information about the characters, setting, or events. Then use Routine 15, Narrative Retelling, to model how to retell the important events in the plot.

COMPREHENSION Compare and Contrast

If...	a student is unable to identify comparisons and contrasts in this selection,
then...	reread the passage with the student and discuss what is being compared and contrasted. Then work with the student to complete a Venn Diagram graphic organizer (p. 122) or T-Chart (p. 125) to list similarities and differences between Joseph and Abona.

VOCABULARY Roots *sect, spect*

If...	a student has trouble identifying the meanings of the words *section* and *spectacular,*
then...	explain the meanings of the roots *sect* (cut) and *spect* (watch or view). Work with the student to give a meaning for each of these words and use each in a sentence: *dissect, insect, spectator, perspective.*

WORD READING Final Syllables *-en, -an, -el*

If...	a student has difficulty correctly reading words with these final syllables,
then...	use Routine 4, Word Parts Strategy, to provide instruction and practice reading the words *even, Americans, morsel, frighten, shaken, historian, Indian, vowel, panel.*

Moving into Instruction 50

SUGGESTED SKILL INSTRUCTION If a student scores below 3 for a skill, use the recommendations below to provide additional instruction for the skill.

RATE

If...	a student scores fewer than 110 wpm on this passage,
then...	identify reading rate difficulties (repetitions, ineffective or slow decoding). Help the student correctly read miscues and eliminate repetitions within a paragraph and then reread the paragraph several times. To provide additional practice, use one of the Fluency Routines, 11–14.

ACCURACY

If...	a student's Record of Oral Reading indicates problems decoding specific word types,
then...	analyze the types of miscues made. Have the student reread a sentence with a miscued word. If the student is unable to decode the miscued word, model and teach how to decode those word types. Then have the student read these types of words in continuous texts.

SUMMARIZE

If...	a student is unable to identify important ideas or details in this passage,
then...	model how to identify an important idea and the details that support it as you read aloud part of the passage. Then have the student do the same with the remainder of the passage. Use Routine 16, Summarizing, for additional instruction and practice.

COMPREHENSION Cause and Effect

If...	a student is unable to identify cause and effect in the text,
then...	use the Cause and Effect graphic organizer (p. 123) to model how to find and record why glaciers are melting. Then, together with the student, record why melting ice might be a problem. Remind the student that a cause-and-effect relationship consists of what happened and why.

VOCABULARY Prefixes and Suffixes *re-, -ly*

If...	a student has trouble determining the meanings of words with *-ly* or *re-*,
then...	explain to the student that the prefix *re-* means "again" and that the suffix *-ly* means "in a certain way." Write the following words: *rethinking, quickly, review, correctly*. With the student, read each word, determine the meaning, and use it in a sentence.

WORD READING Two-Syllable Base Words and Endings with Spelling Changes

If...	the student has difficulty correctly reading two-syllable base words and endings with spelling changes,
then...	use Routine 4, Word Parts Strategy, to provide instruction and practice reading the words *bodies, studies, becoming, beginning, studied, ladies, finishes*.

SUGGESTED SKILL INSTRUCTION If a student scores below 3 for a skill, use the recommendations below to provide additional instruction for the skill.

RATE

If...	a student scores fewer than 110 wpm on this passage,
then...	identify reading rate difficulties (repetitions, ineffective or slow decoding). Help the student correctly read miscues and eliminate repetitions within a paragraph and then reread the paragraph several times. To provide additional practice, use one of the Fluency Routines, 11–14.

ACCURACY

If...	a student's Record of Oral Reading indicates problems decoding specific word types,
then...	analyze the types of miscues made. Have the student reread a sentence with a miscued word. If the student is unable to decode the miscued word, model and teach how to decode those word types. Then have the student read these types of words in continuous texts.

SUMMARIZE

If...	a student is unable to identify important ideas or details in this passage,
then...	model how to identify an important idea and the details that support it as you read aloud part of the passage. Then have the student do the same with the remainder of the passage. Use Routine 16, Summarizing, for additional instruction and practice.

COMPREHENSION Sequence

If...	a student is unable to identify sequence in this selection,
then...	explain that dates can provide clues to sequence. Have the student reread the passage and circle dates in the text, such as *1754–1763* and *1764*. Discuss with the student why understanding sequence is so important to understanding the passage.

VOCABULARY Multiple-Meaning Words

If...	a student cannot identify the appropriate meanings of multiple-meaning words in the selection,
then...	model using different definitions of the word *charge* (to make someone pay; to rush forward in attack; to accuse of a crime) in context and discuss which one makes the most sense in the passage. Then help the student use this method to determine the correct meanings of the words *company, party, matter, side.*

WORD READING Syllable Patterns VCCCV, VCCV, V/CV, V/V

If...	a student has difficulty correctly reading words with these syllable patterns,
then...	use Routine 4, Word Parts Strategy, to provide instruction and practice reading the words *fancy, decided, control, reaction, electric, occurred, company, revolution, decision, reaction, diary.*

SUGGESTED SKILL INSTRUCTION If a student scores below 3 for a skill, use the recommendations below to provide additional instruction for the skill.

RATE

If...	a student scores fewer than 110 wpm on this passage,
then...	identify reading rate difficulties (repetitions, ineffective or slow decoding). Help the student correctly read miscues and eliminate repetitions within a paragraph and then reread the paragraph several times. To provide additional practice, use one of the Fluency Routines, 11–14.

ACCURACY

If...	a student's Record of Oral Reading indicates problems decoding specific word types,
then...	analyze the types of miscues made. Have the student reread a sentence with a miscued word. If the student is unable to decode the miscued word, model and teach how to decode those word types. Then have the student read these types of words in continuous texts.

SUMMARIZE

If...	a student is unable to identify important ideas or details in this passage,
then...	model how to identify an important idea and the details that support it as you read aloud part of the passage. Then have the student do the same with the remainder of the passage. Use Routine 16, Summarizing, for additional instruction and practice.

COMPREHENSION Draw Conclusions

If...	a student is unable to draw conclusions in this selection,
then...	reread the passage together. Then use the Draw Conclusions graphic organizer (p. 124) to model how to use information from the passage to draw a conclusion about Harriet Tubman. Work with the student to draw other conclusions.

VOCABULARY Multiple-Meaning Words

If...	a student cannot identify the appropriate meanings of multiple-meaning words in the selection,
then...	model using different definitions of the word *close* (a short distance away; to shut an opening) in context and discuss which one makes the most sense in the passage. Then help the student use this method to determine the correct meanings of the words *cool*, *times*, *scout*, and *stories*.

WORD READING Multisyllabic Words

If...	a student has difficulty correctly reading multisyllabic words,
then...	use Routine 6, Multisyllabic Word Strategy, for instruction and practice reading the words *slavery*, *courageous*, *enemies*, *bravery*.

Moving into Instruction 50

SUGGESTED SKILL INSTRUCTION If a student scores below 3 for a skill, use the recommendations below to provide additional instruction for the skill.

RATE

If...	a student scores fewer than 115 wpm on this passage,
then...	identify reading rate difficulties (repetitions, ineffective or slow decoding). Help the student correctly read miscues and eliminate repetitions within a paragraph and then reread the paragraph several times. To provide additional practice, use one of the Fluency Routines, 11–14.

ACCURACY

If...	a student's Record of Oral Reading indicates problems decoding specific word types,
then...	analyze the types of miscues made. Have the student reread a sentence with a miscued word. If the student is unable to decode the miscued word, model and teach how to decode those word types. Then have the student read these types of words in continuous texts.

RETELL Character, Setting, and Plot

If...	a student is unable to describe the characters, setting, or most important events in the plot,
then...	use the Character, Setting, and Plot graphic organizer (p. 120) or highlight words or phrases in the story to identify information about the characters, setting, or events. Then use Routine 15, Narrative Retelling, to model how to retell the important events in the plot.

COMPREHENSION Compare and Contrast

If...	a student is unable to compare and contrast characters and events from the story,
then...	explain that when we compare and contrast, we look for similarities and differences. Use two familiar items in the classroom to model how to compare and contrast. Have the student reread the passage and use the T-Chart graphic organizer (p. 125) to list similarities and differences between the teams and the players in the story.

VOCABULARY Roots geo, graph

If...	a student has trouble identifying the meanings of the words *autographed* and *geometric*,
then...	explain the meanings of the roots *graph* (write) and *geo* (earth). Work with the student to give a meaning for each of these words and use each in a sentence: *autograph, geology, graphic, geography, biography.*

WORD READING Greek Roots graph, geo, auto

If...	a student has difficulty correctly reading words with these Greek roots,
then...	use Routine 4, Word Parts Strategy, to provide instruction and practice reading the words *autographed, photographer, geometric, automatic, biography, phonograph, automobile, geology, geometry.*

Moving into Instruction 50

SUGGESTED SKILL INSTRUCTION If a student scores below 3 for a skill, use the recommendations below to provide additional instruction for the skill.

RATE

If...	a student scores fewer than 110 wpm on this passage,
then...	identify reading rate difficulties (repetitions, ineffective or slow decoding). Help the student correctly read miscues and eliminate repetitions within a paragraph and then reread the paragraph several times. To provide additional practice, use one of the Fluency Routines, 11–14.

ACCURACY

If...	a student's Record of Oral Reading indicates problems decoding specific word types,
then...	analyze the types of miscues made. Have the student reread a sentence with a miscued word. If the student is unable to decode the miscued word, model and teach how to decode those word types. Then have the student read these types of words in continuous texts.

SUMMARIZE

If...	a student is unable to identify important ideas or details in this passage,
then...	model how to identify an important idea and the details that support it as you read aloud part of the passage. Then have the student do the same with the remainder of the passage. Use Routine 16, Summarizing, for additional instruction and practice.

COMPREHENSION Draw Conclusions

If...	a student is unable to draw conclusions in this selection,
then...	reread the passage together. Then use the Draw Conclusions graphic organizer (p. 124) to model how to use information from the passage to draw a conclusion about how some sea creatures have adapted to life in the deep ocean. Work with the student to draw other conclusions.

VOCABULARY Multiple-Meaning Words

If...	a student cannot identify the appropriate meanings of multiple-meaning words in the selection,
then...	model using different definitions of the word *mystery* (something unknown; something that needs to be solved) in context and discuss which one makes the most sense in the passage. Then help the student use this method to determine the correct meanings of the words *blend, surface, body*, and *depth*.

WORD READING Suffixes *-ly, -tion, -ion*

If...	a student has difficulty correctly reading words with these suffixes,
then...	use Routine 4, Word Parts Strategy, for instruction and practice reading the words *uniquely, easily, illumination, region, literally*.

Moving into Instruction **50**

SUGGESTED SKILL INSTRUCTION If a student scores below 3 for a skill, use the recommendations below to provide additional instruction for the skill.

RATE

If...	a student scores fewer than 115 wpm on this passage,
then...	identify reading rate difficulties (repetitions, ineffective or slow decoding). Help the student correctly read miscues and eliminate repetitions within a paragraph and then reread the paragraph several times. To provide additional practice, use one of the Fluency Routines, 11–14.

ACCURACY

If...	a student's Record of Oral Reading indicates problems decoding specific word types,
then...	analyze the types of miscues made. Have the student reread a sentence with a miscued word. If the student is unable to decode the miscued word, model and teach how to decode those word types. Then have the student read these types of words in continuous texts.

RETELL Character, Setting, and Plot

If...	a student is unable to describe the characters, setting, or most important events in the plot,
then...	use the Character, Setting, and Plot graphic organizer (p. 120) or highlight words or phrases in the story to identify information about the characters, setting, or events. Then use Routine 15, Narrative Retelling, to model how to retell the important events in the plot.

COMPREHENSION Draw Conclusions

If...	a student is unable to draw conclusions in this selection,
then...	reread the passage together. Then use the Draw Conclusions graphic organizer (p. 124) to model how to use information from the passage to draw a conclusion about what Alex is delivering for Ben Franklin. Work with the student to draw other conclusions.

VOCABULARY Context Clues

If...	a student has trouble identifying word meanings using context clues,
then...	point out specific words and phrases that provide clues to the meaning of the word *apprentice,* such as "...my employer... an apprentice in his print shop." Then help the student figure out the meanings of *leaflet* and *mission* by finding words or phrases that provide clues to their meanings.

WORD READING Long Vowel Digraphs *ea, ee, ei*

If...	a student has difficulty correctly reading words with these long vowel digraphs,
then...	use Routine 2, Whole-Word Blending, to provide instruction and practice reading the words *neighbor, leaflet, freedom, seekers, conceal, soybeans, agreement, eighteen.*

Moving into Instruction 50

SUGGESTED SKILL INSTRUCTION If a student scores below 3 for a skill, use the recommendations below to provide additional instruction for the skill.

RATE	
If...	a student scores fewer than 115 wpm on this passage,
then...	identify reading rate difficulties (repetitions, ineffective or slow decoding). Help the student correctly read miscues and eliminate repetitions within a paragraph and then reread the paragraph several times. To provide additional practice, use one of the Fluency Routines, 11–14.

ACCURACY	
If...	a student's Record of Oral Reading indicates problems decoding specific word types,
then...	analyze the types of miscues made. Have the student reread a sentence with a miscued word. If the student is unable to decode the miscued word, model and teach how to decode those word types. Then have the student read these types of words in continuous texts.

RETELL Character, Setting, and Plot	
If...	a student is unable to describe the characters, setting, or most important events in the plot,
then...	use the Character, Setting, and Plot graphic organizer (p. 120) or highlight words or phrases in the story to identify information about the characters, setting, or events. Then use Routine 15, Narrative Retelling, to model how to retell the important events in the plot.

COMPREHENSION Cause and Effect	
If...	a student is unable to identify cause and effect in the text,
then...	use the Cause and Effect graphic organizer (p. 123) to model how to find and record what the chain reaction is. Then, together with the student, record additional causes and effects from the selection.

VOCABULARY Context Clues	
If...	a student has trouble identifying word meanings using context clues,
then...	point out specific words and phrases that provide clues to the meaning of *chain reaction*, such as "… when the marble reached the end of the track, it started a chain reaction of the dominoes." Then help the student figure out the meanings of *humorous* and *switch* by finding words or phrases that provide clues to their meanings.

WORD READING Common Syllables *-sure, -ious, -ous*	
If...	a student has difficulty correctly reading words with these common syllables,
then...	use Routine 6, Multisyllabic Word Strategy, to provide instruction and practice reading the words *assure, serious, humorous, mysterious, previous, exposure, pleasure, dangerous, numerous.*

Moving into Instruction **50**

SUGGESTED SKILL INSTRUCTION If a student scores below 3 for a skill, use the recommendations below to provide additional instruction for the skill.

RATE

If...	a student scores fewer than 110 wpm on this passage,
then...	identify reading rate difficulties (repetitions, ineffective or slow decoding). Help the student correctly read miscues and eliminate repetitions within a paragraph and then reread the paragraph several times. To provide additional practice, use one of the Fluency Routines, 11–14.

ACCURACY

If...	a student's Record of Oral Reading indicates problems decoding specific word types,
then...	analyze the types of miscues made. Have the student reread a sentence with a miscued word. If the student is unable to decode the miscued word, model and teach how to decode those word types. Then have the student read these types of words in continuous texts.

SUMMARIZE

If...	a student is unable to identify important ideas or details in this passage,
then...	model how to identify an important idea and the details that support it as you read aloud part of the passage. Then have the student do the same with the remainder of the passage. Use Routine 16, Summarizing, for additional instruction and practice.

COMPREHENSION Sequence

If...	a student is unable to identify sequence in this selection,
then...	explain how to use signal words to determine sequence. Have the student reread the passage, underlining signal words such as *first, then,* and *finally.* Have the student use this information to complete a Sequence–Nonfiction graphic organizer (p. 119).

VOCABULARY Prefixes and Suffixes *over-, -ly*

If...	a student has trouble determining the meanings of words with *-ly* or *over-,*
then...	explain to the student that the prefix *over-* means "extra" or "too much" and that the suffix *-ly* means "in a certain way." Write the following words: *wisely, overextending, perfectly, overthrow.* With the student, read each word, determine the meaning, and use it in a sentence.

WORD READING Prefixes *re-, semi-, over-*

If...	a student has difficulty correctly reading words with these prefixes,
then...	use Routine 4, Word Parts Strategy, for instruction and practice reading the words *overextending, returns, semicircular, overboard, overturn, remove, reorganize, semicolon, semisweet.*

SUGGESTED SKILL INSTRUCTION If a student scores below 3 for a skill, use the recommendations below to provide additional instruction for the skill.

RATE	
If...	a student scores fewer than 110 wpm on this passage,
then...	identify reading rate difficulties (repetitions, ineffective or slow decoding). Help the student correctly read miscues and eliminate repetitions within a paragraph and then reread the paragraph several times. To provide additional practice, use one of the Fluency Routines, 11–14.

ACCURACY	
If...	a student's Record of Oral Reading indicates problems decoding specific word types,
then...	analyze the types of miscues made. Have the student reread a sentence with a miscued word. If the student is unable to decode the miscued word, model and teach how to decode those word types. Then have the student read these types of words in continuous texts.

SUMMARIZE	
If...	a student is unable to identify important ideas or details in this passage,
then...	model how to identify an important idea and the details that support it as you read aloud part of the passage. Then have the student do the same with the remainder of the passage. Use Routine 16, Summarizing, for additional instruction and practice.

COMPREHENSION Compare and Contrast	
If...	a student is unable to identify comparisons and contrasts in this passage,
then...	discuss with the student what is being compared and contrasted in this passage. Have the student identify how robots in books and movies and robots in real life are alike and different and use a Venn Diagram graphic organizer (p. 122) to list this information.

VOCABULARY Prefixes and Suffixes *im-, -ous*	
If...	a student has trouble determining the meanings of words with *im-* or *-ous*,
then...	explain to the student that the prefix *im-* means "not" and that the suffix *-ous* means "full of." Write the following words: *impossible, dangerous, immovable, famous*. With the student, read each word, determine the meaning, and use it in a sentence.

WORD READING Suffixes *-ize, -ate*	
If...	a student has difficulty correctly reading words with these suffixes,
then...	use Routine 6, Multisyllabic Word Strategy, for instruction and practice reading the words *vocalize, mechanized, operate, activate, apologize, energize, memorize, calculate, celebrate, elevate, illustrate*.

Moving into Instruction 50

SUGGESTED SKILL INSTRUCTION If a student scores below 3 for a skill, use the recommendations below to provide additional instruction for the skill.

RATE

If...	a student scores fewer than 110 wpm on this passage,
then...	identify reading rate difficulties (repetitions, ineffective or slow decoding). Help the student correctly read miscues and eliminate repetitions within a paragraph and then reread the paragraph several times. To provide additional practice, use one of the Fluency Routines, 11–14.

ACCURACY

If...	a student's Record of Oral Reading indicates problems decoding specific word types,
then...	analyze the types of miscues made. Have the student reread a sentence with a miscued word. If the student is unable to decode the miscued word, model and teach how to decode those word types. Then have the student read these types of words in continuous texts.

SUMMARIZE

If...	a student is unable to identify important ideas or details in this passage,
then...	model how to identify an important idea and the details that support it as you read aloud part of the passage. Then have the student do the same with the remainder of the passage. Use Routine 16, Summarizing, for additional instruction and practice.

COMPREHENSION Cause and Effect

If...	a student is unable to identify cause and effect in the text,
then...	use a Cause and Effect graphic organizer (p. 123) to model how to find out what caused many people to come to America. Record it on the chart. With the student, record what happened because immigrants had to learn a new language. Record another cause-and-effect relationship from the passage.

VOCABULARY Context Clues

If...	a student has trouble identifying word meanings using context clues,
then...	point out specific words and phrases that provide clues to the meaning of *immigrants,* such as "Some ... were welcomed... started to arrive from other countries. ..." Then help the student figure out the meanings of *exchange* and *expanding* by finding words or phrases that provide clues to their meanings.

WORD READING Prefixes *de-, ex-, ir-*

If...	a student has difficulty correctly reading words with these prefixes,
then...	use Routine 4, Word Parts Strategy, for instruction and practice reading the words *expanding, irresistible, exchange, despite, decrease, excite, extreme, exclaim, irregular, irresponsible.*

Moving into Instruction 50

SUGGESTED SKILL INSTRUCTION If a student scores below 3 for a skill, use the recommendations below to provide additional instruction for the skill.

RATE

If...	a student scores fewer than 115 wpm on this passage,
then...	identify reading rate difficulties (repetitions, ineffective or slow decoding). Help the student correctly read miscues and eliminate repetitions within a paragraph and then reread the paragraph several times. To provide additional practice, use one of the Fluency Routines, 11–14.

ACCURACY

If...	a student's Record of Oral Reading indicates problems decoding specific word types,
then...	analyze the types of miscues made. Have the student reread a sentence with a miscued word. If the student is unable to decode the miscued word, model and teach how to decode those word types. Then have the student read these types of words in continuous texts.

RETELL Character, Setting, and Plot

If...	a student is unable to describe the characters, setting, or most important events in the plot,
then...	use the Character, Setting, and Plot graphic organizer (p. 120) or highlight words or phrases in the story to identify information about the characters, setting, or events. Then use Routine 15, Narrative Retelling, to model how to retell the important events in the plot.

COMPREHENSION Draw Conclusions

If...	a student is unable to draw conclusions in this selection,
then...	reread the passage together. Then use the Draw Conclusions graphic organizer (p. 124) to model how to use information from the passage to draw a conclusion about whether or not they think Eddie will get a part in the play and why. Work with the student to draw other conclusions.

VOCABULARY Context Clues

If...	a student has trouble identifying word meanings using context clues,
then...	point out specific words and phrases that provide clues to the meaning of the word *expressive*, such as "an expressive voice—it makes people really feel the music." Then help the student figure out the meanings of *intensity* and *ambitious* by finding words or phrases that provide clues to their meanings.

WORD READING Common Syllables *-tive, -sive, -ify, -ity*

If...	a student has difficulty correctly reading words with these common syllables,
then...	use Routine 6, Multisyllabic Word Strategy, for instruction and practice reading the words *talkative, expressive, terrify, intensity, attentive, inventive, intensive, horrify, magnify, ability, captivity, generosity.*

Moving into Instruction **50**

SUGGESTED SKILL INSTRUCTION If a student scores below 3 for a skill, use the recommendations below to provide additional instruction for the skill.

RATE

If...	a student scores fewer than 115 wpm on this passage,
then...	identify reading rate difficulties (repetitions, ineffective or slow decoding). Help the student correctly read miscues and eliminate repetitions within a paragraph and then reread the paragraph several times. To provide additional practice, use one of the Fluency Routines, 11–14.

ACCURACY

If...	a student's Record of Oral Reading indicates problems decoding specific word types,
then...	analyze the types of miscues made. Have the student reread a sentence with a miscued word. If the student is unable to decode the miscued word, model and teach how to decode those word types. Then have the student read these types of words in continuous texts.

RETELL Character, Setting, and Plot

If...	a student is unable to describe the characters, setting, or most important events in the plot,
then...	use the Character, Setting, and Plot graphic organizer (p. 120) or highlight words or phrases in the story to identify information about the characters, setting, or events. Then use Routine 15, Narrative Retelling, to model how to retell the important events in the plot.

COMPREHENSION Draw Conclusions

If...	a student is unable to draw conclusions in this selection,
then...	reread the passage together. Then use the Draw Conclusions graphic organizer (p. 124) to model how to use information from the passage to draw a conclusion about whether or not Kim's restaurant will be a success and why. Work with the student to draw other conclusions.

VOCABULARY Roots *dict, scrib*

If...	a student has trouble identifying the meanings of the words *dictated* and *describe*,
then...	explain the meanings of the roots *dict* (say or speak) and *scrib* (write). Work with the student to give a meaning for each of these words and use each in a sentence: *dictionary, predict, inscribe, subscribe.*

WORD READING Latin Roots *dict, scrib, vis*

If...	a student has difficulty correctly reading words with these Latin roots,
then...	use Routine 6, Multisyllabic Word Strategy, for instruction and practice reading the words *supervised, describe, predict, visited, dictate, predict, subscribe, prescription, envision, visible, visitor.*

SUGGESTED SKILL INSTRUCTION If a student scores below 3 for a skill, use the recommendations below to provide additional instruction for the skill.

RATE

If...	a student scores fewer than 110 wpm on this passage,
then...	identify reading rate difficulties (repetitions, ineffective or slow decoding). Help the student correctly read miscues and eliminate repetitions within a paragraph and then reread the paragraph several times. To provide additional practice, use one of the Fluency Routines, 11–14.

ACCURACY

If...	a student's Record of Oral Reading indicates problems decoding specific word types,
then...	analyze the types of miscues made. Have the student reread a sentence with a miscued word. If the student is unable to decode the miscued word, model and teach how to decode those word types. Then have the student read these types of words in continuous texts.

SUMMARIZE

If...	a student is unable to identify important ideas or details in this passage,
then...	model how to identify an important idea and the details that support it as you read aloud part of the passage. Then have the student do the same with the remainder of the passage. Use Routine 16, Summarizing, for additional instruction and practice.

COMPREHENSION Sequence

If...	a student is unable to identify sequence in this selection,
then...	have the student reread the passage and list the events in paragraph two that describe the birth of a star. Then ask the student to complete the Sequence–Nonfiction graphic organizer (p. 119) and explain why the sequence of events is important to understanding this passage.

VOCABULARY Multiple-Meaning Words

If...	a student cannot identify the appropriate meanings of multiple-meaning words in the selection,
then...	model using different definitions of the word *star* (a fixed point of light in the night sky; a famous, talented person) in context and discuss which one makes the most sense in the passage. Then help the student use this method to determine the correct meanings of the words *grain* and *make*.

WORD READING Multisyllabic Words

If...	a student has difficulty correctly reading multisyllabic words,
then...	use Routine 6, Multisyllabic Word Strategy, for instruction and practice reading the words *visible, nurseries, medium, galaxy, universe*.

Moving into Instruction **50**

SUGGESTED SKILL INSTRUCTION If a student scores below 3 for a skill, use the recommendations below to provide additional instruction for the skill.

RATE

If...	a student scores fewer than 120 wpm on this passage,
then...	identify reading rate difficulties (repetitions, ineffective or slow decoding). Help the student correctly read miscues and eliminate repetitions within a paragraph and then reread the paragraph several times. To provide additional practice, use one of the Fluency Routines, 11–14.

ACCURACY

If...	a student's Record of Oral Reading indicates problems decoding specific word types,
then...	analyze the types of miscues made. Have the student reread a sentence with a miscued word. If the student is unable to decode the miscued word, model and teach how to decode those word types. Then have the student read these types of words in continuous texts.

SUMMARIZE

If...	a student is unable to identify important ideas or details in this passage,
then...	model how to identify an important idea and the details that support it as you read aloud part of the passage. Then have the student do the same with the remainder of the passage. Use Routine 16, Summarizing, for additional instruction and practice.

COMPREHENSION Sequence

If...	a student is unable to identify sequence in this selection,
then...	have the student read the passage aloud and then identify clue words and phrases that signal sequence (such as *first, next, after, afterward, the last step, finally.*) Then have the student complete a Sequence–Nonfiction graphic organizer (p. 119). Ask the student to explain why the sequence, or order of steps, described in this passage is so important to the reader's understanding of the text.

VOCABULARY Prefixes and Suffixes *dis-, -like*

If...	a student has trouble determining the meanings of words with *-like* or *dis-*,
then...	explain to the student that the prefix *dis-* means "not," "opposite of," or "harm or make bad," and that the suffix *-like* means "similar to." Write the following words: *saplike, disfigure, disable, dreamlike.* With the student, read each word, determine the meaning, and use it in a sentence.

WORD READING Multisyllabic Words

If...	a student has difficulty correctly reading multisyllabic words,
then...	use Routine 6, Multisyllabic Word Strategy, for instruction and practice reading the words *procedure, mummification, ritual, emotions.*

SUGGESTED SKILL INSTRUCTION If a student scores below 3 for a skill, use the recommendations below to provide additional instruction for the skill.

RATE

If...	a student scores fewer than 125 wpm on this passage,
then...	identify reading rate difficulties (repetitions, ineffective or slow decoding). Help the student correctly read miscues and eliminate repetitions within a paragraph and then reread the paragraph several times. To provide additional practice, use one of the Fluency Routines, 11–14.

ACCURACY

If...	a student's Record of Oral Reading indicates problems decoding specific word types,
then...	analyze the types of miscues made. Have the student reread a sentence with a miscued word. If the student is unable to decode the miscued word, model and teach how to decode those word types. Then have the student read these types of words in continuous texts.

RETELL Character, Setting, and Plot

If...	a student is unable to describe the characters, setting, or most important events in the plot,
then...	use the Character, Setting, and Plot graphic organizer (p. 120) or highlight words or phrases in the story to identify information about the characters, setting, or events. Then use Routine 15, Narrative Retelling, to model how to retell the important events in the plot.

COMPREHENSION Cause and Effect

If...	a student is unable to identify cause and effect in the text,
then...	use the Cause and Effect graphic organizer (p. 123) to model how to find out why Sally and her friend do not like camping. Record it on the chart. Then, together with the student, record why the girls get scared. Remind the student that a cause-and-effect relationship consists of what happened and why.

VOCABULARY Context Clues

If...	a student has trouble identifying word meanings using context clues,
then...	point out specific words and phrases that provide clues to the meaning of the word *huddled,* such as "...huddled around the campfire. ..." Then help the student figure out meanings of the words *flickered* and *taunting* by finding words or phrases that provide clues to their meanings.

WORD READING Multisyllabic Words

If...	a student has difficulty correctly reading multisyllabic words,
then...	use Routine 6, Multisyllabic Word Strategy, for instruction and practice reading the words *barriers, abandon, hysterical, accompanied.*

Moving into Instruction 60

SUGGESTED SKILL INSTRUCTION If a student scores below 3 for a skill, use the recommendations below to provide additional instruction for the skill.

RATE

If...	a student scores fewer than 120 wpm on this passage,
then...	identify reading rate difficulties (repetitions, ineffective or slow decoding). Help the student correctly read miscues and eliminate repetitions within a paragraph and then reread the paragraph several times. To provide additional practice, use one of the Fluency Routines, 11–14.

ACCURACY

If...	a student's Record of Oral Reading indicates problems decoding specific word types,
then...	analyze the types of miscues made. Have the student reread a sentence with a miscued word. If the student is unable to decode the miscued word, model and teach how to decode those word types. Then have the student read these types of words in continuous texts.

SUMMARIZE

If...	a student is unable to identify important ideas or details in this passage,
then...	model how to identify an important idea and the details that support it as you read aloud part of the passage. Then have the student do the same with the remainder of the passage. Use Routine 16, Summarizing, for additional instruction and practice.

COMPREHENSION Sequence

If...	a student is unable to identify sequence in this selection,
then...	have the student read the passage aloud. Remind him or her that it is possible to identify sequence in text without clue words. Then help the student complete a Sequence–Nonfiction graphic organizer (p. 119). Ask the student to explain why the sequence, or order of steps, described in paragraph four of the passage is so important to the reader's understanding of the text.

VOCABULARY Compound Words

If...	a student has trouble identifying the meanings of compound words,
then...	model using the smaller words in the word *sweatshop* to figure out what the word means. Then ask the student to use the same routine to find the meaning of *foreman*.

WORD READING Common Syllables -ive, -sive, ify, -ity

If...	a student has difficulty correctly reading words with these common syllables,
then...	use Routine 4, Word Parts Strategy, to provide instruction and practice reading the words *intensify*, *excessive*, *majority*, *abusive*, *adhesive*, *deductive*, *certify*, *clarity*, *perceptive*, *simplify*.

Moving into Instruction 60

SUGGESTED SKILL INSTRUCTION If a student scores below 3 for a skill, use the recommendations below to provide additional instruction for the skill.

RATE

If...	a student scores fewer than 125 wpm on this passage,
then...	identify reading rate difficulties (repetitions, ineffective or slow decoding). Help the student correctly read miscues and eliminate repetitions within a paragraph and then reread the paragraph several times. To provide additional practice, use one of the Fluency Routines, 11–14.

ACCURACY

If...	a student's Record of Oral Reading indicates problems decoding specific word types,
then...	analyze the types of miscues made. Have the student reread a sentence with a miscued word. If the student is unable to decode the miscued word, model and teach how to decode those word types. Then have the student read these types of words in continuous texts.

RETELL Character, Setting, and Plot

If...	a student is unable to describe the characters, setting, or most important events in the plot,
then...	use the Character, Setting, and Plot graphic organizer (p. 120) or highlight words or phrases in the story to identify information about the characters, setting, or events. Then use Routine 15, Narrative Retelling, to model how to retell the important events in the plot.

COMPREHENSION Compare and Contrast

If...	a student is unable to identify comparisons and contrasts in this selection,
then...	have the student reread the passage and ask him or her what features described in this passage are being compared and contrasted. Then help the student complete a T-Chart graphic organizer (p. 125) to record how Mike felt about his brother at the beginning of the story versus how he felt at the end.

VOCABULARY Context Clues

If...	a student has trouble identifying word meanings using context clues,
then...	point out specific words and phrases that provide clues to the meaning of the word *unison,* such as "...Lee and Kenny both chanted in unison." Then help the student figure out the meanings of the words *fervor* and *agony* by finding words or phrases that provide clues to their meanings.

WORD READING Latin Roots *inter, uni*

If...	a student has difficulty correctly reading words with these Latin roots,
then...	use Routine 4, Word Parts Strategy, to provide instruction and practice reading the words *unison, intercept, interception, unity, unify, interact, intercom, interfere.*

Moving into Instruction **60**

SUGGESTED SKILL INSTRUCTION If a student scores below 3 for a skill, use the recommendations below to provide additional instruction for the skill.

RATE

If...	a student scores fewer than 120 wpm on this passage,
then...	identify reading rate difficulties (repetitions, ineffective or slow decoding). Help the student correctly read miscues and eliminate repetitions within a paragraph and then reread the paragraph several times. To provide additional practice, use one of the Fluency Routines, 11–14.

ACCURACY

If...	a student's Record of Oral Reading indicates problems decoding specific word types,
then...	analyze the types of miscues made. Have the student reread a sentence with a miscued word. If the student is unable to decode the miscued word, model and teach how to decode those word types. Then have the student read these types of words in continuous texts.

SUMMARIZE

If...	a student is unable to identify important ideas or details in this passage,
then...	model how to identify an important idea and the details that support it as you read aloud part of the passage. Then have the student do the same with the remainder of the passage. Use Routine 16, Summarizing, for additional instruction and practice.

COMPREHENSION Draw Conclusions

If...	a student is unable to draw conclusions in this selection,
then...	reread the passage together. Then use the Draw Conclusions graphic organizer (p. 124) to model how to use information from the passage to draw a conclusion about one way that GPS is useful. Work with the student to draw other conclusions.

VOCABULARY Multiple-Meaning Words

If...	a student cannot identify the appropriate meanings of multiple-meaning words in the selection,
then...	model using different definitions of the word *address* (where someone lives; to speak to someone) in context and discuss which one makes the most sense in the passage. Then help the student use this method to determine the correct meanings of the words *figures, receiver,* and *ground.*

WORD READING Suffixes *-less, -ship, -ence*

If...	a student has difficulty correctly reading words with these suffixes,
then...	use Routine 4, Word Parts Strategy, to provide instruction and practice reading the words *clueless, hardship, convenience, blameless, flawless, audience, turbulence, membership, workmanship.*

SUGGESTED SKILL INSTRUCTION If a student scores below 3 for a skill, use the recommendations below to provide additional instruction for the skill.

RATE

If...	a student scores fewer than 125 wpm on this passage,
then...	identify reading rate difficulties (repetitions, ineffective or slow decoding). Help the student correctly read miscues and eliminate repetitions within a paragraph and then reread the paragraph several times. To provide additional practice, use one of the Fluency Routines, 11–14.

ACCURACY

If...	a student's Record of Oral Reading indicates problems decoding specific word types,
then...	analyze the types of miscues made. Have the student reread a sentence with a miscued word. If the student is unable to decode the miscued word, model and teach how to decode those word types. Then have the student read these types of words in continuous texts.

RETELL Character, Setting, and Plot

If...	a student is unable to describe the characters, setting, or most important events in the plot,
then...	use the Character, Setting, and Plot graphic organizer (p. 120) or highlight words or phrases in the story to identify information about the characters, setting, or events. Then use Routine 15, Narrative Retelling, to model how to retell the important events in the plot.

COMPREHENSION Draw Conclusions

If...	a student is unable to draw conclusions in this selection,
then...	reread the passage together. Then use the Draw Conclusions graphic organizer (p. 124) to model how to use information from the passage to draw a conclusion about Jaime's feelings and ideas. Work with the student to draw other conclusions.

VOCABULARY Context Clues

If...	a student has trouble identifying word meanings using context clues,
then...	point out specific words and phrases that provide clues to the meaning of the word *tempo*, such as "...the tempo of the game was so rapid. ..." Then help the student figure out the meanings of the words *sympathized* and *scrimmages* by finding words or phrases that provide clues to their meanings.

WORD READING Latin Roots *temp, clin, pul, mar, vit*

If...	a student has difficulty correctly reading words with these Latin roots,
then...	use Routine 4, Word Parts Strategy, to provide instruction and practice reading the words *tempo, inclined, impulse, submarine, vital, temperature, clinic, impulsive, maritime, vitamin*.

Moving into Instruction **60**

SUGGESTED SKILL INSTRUCTION If a student scores below 3 for a skill, use the recommendations below to provide additional instruction for the skill.

RATE

If...	a student scores fewer than 120 wpm on this passage,
then...	identify reading rate difficulties (repetitions, ineffective or slow decoding). Help the student correctly read miscues and eliminate repetitions within a paragraph and then reread the paragraph several times. To provide additional practice, use one of the Fluency Routines, 11–14.

ACCURACY

If...	a student's Record of Oral Reading indicates problems decoding specific word types,
then...	analyze the types of miscues made. Have the student reread a sentence with a miscued word. If the student is unable to decode the miscued word, model and teach how to decode those word types. Then have the student read these types of words in continuous texts.

SUMMARIZE

If...	a student is unable to identify important ideas or details in this passage,
then...	model how to identify an important idea and the details that support it as you read aloud part of the passage. Then have the student do the same with the remainder of the passage. Use Routine 16, Summarizing, for additional instruction and practice.

COMPREHENSION Draw Conclusions

If...	a student is unable to draw conclusions in this selection,
then...	reread the passage together. Then use the Draw Conclusions graphic organizer (p. 124) to model how to use information from the passage to draw a conclusion about the discovery in the cave. Work with the student to draw other conclusions.

VOCABULARY Context Clues

If...	a student has trouble identifying word meanings using context clues,
then...	point out specific words and phrases that provide clues to the meaning of the word *expedition*, such as "went on an expedition...a cave that was near their home. ..." Then help the student figure out the meanings of the words *bedrock* and *awestruck* by finding words or phrases that provide clues to their meanings.

WORD READING Multisyllabic Words

If...	a student has difficulty correctly reading multisyllabic words,
then...	use Routine 6, Multisyllabic Word Strategy, for instruction and practice reading the words *expedition, archaeologist, pictographs, collection*.

Moving into Instruction 60

SUGGESTED SKILL INSTRUCTION If a student scores below 3 for a skill, use the recommendations below to provide additional instruction for the skill.

RATE

If...	a student scores fewer than 120 wpm on this passage,
then...	identify reading rate difficulties (repetitions, ineffective or slow decoding). Help the student correctly read miscues and eliminate repetitions within a paragraph and then reread the paragraph several times. To provide additional practice, use one of the Fluency Routines, 11–14.

ACCURACY

If...	a student's Record of Oral Reading indicates problems decoding specific word types,
then...	analyze the types of miscues made. Have the student reread a sentence with a miscued word. If the student is unable to decode the miscued word, model and teach how to decode those word types. Then have the student read these types of words in continuous texts.

SUMMARIZE

If...	a student is unable to identify important ideas or details in this passage,
then...	model how to identify an important idea and the details that support it as you read aloud part of the passage. Then have the student do the same with the remainder of the passage. Use Routine 16, Summarizing, for additional instruction and practice.

COMPREHENSION Cause and Effect

If...	a student is unable to identify cause and effect in this selection,
then...	have the student identify clue words and phrases that signal cause and effect, such as reasons. Then have the student use a Cause and Effect graphic organizer (p. 123) to write a short description of two events in the passage, explaining what happened and why it happened.

VOCABULARY Multiple-Meaning Words

If...	a student cannot identify the appropriate meanings of multiple-meaning words in the selection,
then...	model using different definitions of the word *capital* (an uppercase letter; a place where a government is located) in context and discuss which one makes the most sense in the passage. Then help the student use this method to determine the correct meanings of the words *objects, trapped, area,* and *codes.*

WORD READING Syllable Patterns VCV, VCCV, C + *le*, VCCCV, V/V

If...	a student has difficulty correctly reading words with these syllable patterns,
then...	use Routine 4, Word Parts Strategy, to provide instruction and practice reading the words *creating, epicenter, people, cardboard, destroyed, violent.*

Moving into Instruction 60

SUGGESTED SKILL INSTRUCTION If a student scores below 3 for a skill, use the recommendations below to provide additional instruction for the skill.

RATE

If...	a student scores fewer than 120 wpm on this passage,
then...	identify reading rate difficulties (repetitions, ineffective or slow decoding). Help the student correctly read miscues and eliminate repetitions within a paragraph and then reread the paragraph several times. To provide additional practice, use one of the Fluency Routines, 11–14.

ACCURACY

If...	a student's Record of Oral Reading indicates problems decoding specific word types,
then...	analyze the types of miscues made. Have the student reread a sentence with a miscued word. If the student is unable to decode the miscued word, model and teach how to decode those word types. Then have the student read these types of words in continuous texts.

SUMMARIZE

If...	a student is unable to identify important ideas or details in this passage,
then...	model how to identify an important idea and the details that support it as you read aloud part of the passage. Then have the student do the same with the remainder of the passage. Use Routine 16, Summarizing, for additional instruction and practice.

COMPREHENSION Draw Conclusions

If...	a student is unable to draw conclusions in this selection,
then...	reread the passage together. Then use the Draw Conclusions graphic organizer (p. 124) to model how to use information from the passage to draw a conclusion about the accomplishments of the Incas. Work with the student to draw other conclusions.

VOCABULARY Multiple-Meaning Words

If...	a student cannot identify the appropriate meanings of multiple-meaning words in the selection,
then...	model using different definitions of the word *grain* (a cereal crop; small piece of something) in context and discuss which one makes the most sense in the passage. Then help the student use this method to determine the correct meanings of the words *remain, left, track,* and *unravel.*

WORD READING Greek and Latin Roots *geo, sy , civ*

If...	a student has difficulty correctly reading words with these Greek and Latin roots,
then...	use Routine 4, Word Parts Strategy, to provide instruction and practice reading the words *geometry, symbol, civilization, geology, geography, syllable, symmetry, civilized, civil.*

Moving into Instruction 60

SUGGESTED SKILL INSTRUCTION If a student scores below 3 for a skill, use the recommendations below to provide additional instruction for the skill.

RATE

If...	a student scores fewer than 125 wpm on this passage,
then...	identify reading rate difficulties (repetitions, ineffective or slow decoding). Help the student correctly read miscues and eliminate repetitions within a paragraph and then reread the paragraph several times. To provide additional practice, use one of the Fluency Routines, 11–14.

ACCURACY

If...	a student's Record of Oral Reading indicates problems decoding specific word types,
then...	analyze the types of miscues made. Have the student reread a sentence with a miscued word. If the student is unable to decode the miscued word, model and teach how to decode those word types. Then have the student read these types of words in continuous texts.

RETELL Character, Setting, and Plot

If...	a student is unable to describe the characters, setting, or most important events in the plot,
then...	use the Character, Setting, and Plot graphic organizer (p. 120) or highlight words or phrases in the story to identify information about the characters, setting, or events. Then use Routine 15, Narrative Retelling, to model how to retell the important events in the plot.

COMPREHENSION Compare and Contrast

If...	a student is unable to identify comparisons and contrasts in this selection,
then...	have the student reread the passage and ask him or her what features described in this passage are being compared and contrasted. Then help the student complete a Venn Diagram graphic organizer (p. 122) to chart similarities and differences between two of the animals that were observed on the safari.

VOCABULARY Roots *therm, sym*

If...	a student has trouble identifying the meanings of the words *thermos* and *symphony,*
then...	explain the meanings of the roots *therm* (heat) and *sym* (with). Work with the student to give a meaning for each of these words and use each in a sentence: *thermal, thermometer, sympathy.*

WORD READING Common Syllables

If...	a student has difficulty correctly reading words with common syllables,
then...	use Routine 4, Word Parts Strategy, to provide instruction and practice reading the words *adventure, attention, pleasure, agriculture, manufacture, measure, composure, section, notation.*

Moving into Instruction **60**

SUGGESTED SKILL INSTRUCTION If a student scores below 3 for a skill, use the recommendations below to provide additional instruction for the skill.

RATE

If...	a student scores fewer than 125 wpm on this passage,
then...	identify reading rate difficulties (repetitions, ineffective or slow decoding). Help the student correctly read miscues and eliminate repetitions within a paragraph and then reread the paragraph several times. To provide additional practice, use one of the Fluency Routines, 11–14.

ACCURACY

If...	a student's Record of Oral Reading indicates problems decoding specific word types,
then...	analyze the types of miscues made. Have the student reread a sentence with a miscued word. If the student is unable to decode the miscued word, model and teach how to decode those word types. Then have the student read these types of words in continuous texts.

RETELL Character, Setting, and Plot

If...	a student is unable to describe the characters, setting, or most important events in the plot,
then...	use the Character, Setting, and Plot graphic organizer (p. 120) or highlight words or phrases in the story to identify information about the characters, setting, or events. Then use Routine 15, Narrative Retelling, to model how to retell the important events in the plot.

COMPREHENSION Sequence

If...	a student is unable to identify sequence in this selection,
then...	ask the student to circle signal words and phrases for sequence in the text, such as _then, after, when, in just a few hours._ Ask the student to explain how the sequence, or order of events, led to the final result of the story.

VOCABULARY Context Clues

If...	a student has trouble identifying word meanings using context clues,
then...	point out specific words and phrases that provide clues to the meaning of the word _samurai,_ such as "…warrior…swords…soldiers in uniform…" Then help the student figure out the meanings of the words _astonished_ and _virtue_ by finding words or phrases that provide clues to their meanings.

WORD READING Prefixes _dis-, uni-, pro-_

If...	a student has difficulty correctly reading words with these prefixes,
then...	use Routine 4, Word Parts Strategy, to provide instruction and practice reading the words _dishonor, proclaimed, uniform, disgrace, proceed, disagreeable, proclaim, uniformity, university._

Moving into Instruction 60

SUGGESTED SKILL INSTRUCTION If a student scores below 3 for a skill, use the recommendations below to provide additional instruction for the skill.

RATE

If...	a student scores fewer than 125 wpm on this passage,
then...	identify reading rate difficulties (repetitions, ineffective or slow decoding). Help the student correctly read miscues and eliminate repetitions within a paragraph and then reread the paragraph several times. To provide additional practice, use one of the Fluency Routines, 11–14.

ACCURACY

If...	a student's Record of Oral Reading indicates problems decoding specific word types,
then...	analyze the types of miscues made. Have the student reread a sentence with a miscued word. If the student is unable to decode the miscued word, model and teach how to decode those word types. Then have the student read these types of words in continuous texts.

RETELL Character, Setting, and Plot

If...	a student is unable to describe the characters, setting, or most important events in the plot,
then...	use the Character, Setting, and Plot graphic organizer (p. 120) or highlight words or phrases in the story to identify information about the characters, setting, or events. Then use Routine 15, Narrative Retelling, to model how to retell the important events in the plot.

COMPREHENSION Cause and Effect

If...	a student is unable to identify cause and effect in the text,
then...	use the Cause and Effect graphic organizer (p. 123) to model how to find out why Li agrees to keep his promise to Rico at first. Record it on the chart. Then, together with the student, record why Li decides to tell the coach. Remind the student that a cause-and-effect relationship consists of what happened and why.

VOCABULARY Roots *tempor, mal*

If...	a student has trouble identifying the meanings of the words *temporary* and *dismal*,
then...	explain the meanings of the roots *tempor* (time) and *mal* (bad). Work with the student to give a meaning for each of these words and use each in a sentence: *contemporary, malcontent, malnutrition.*

WORD READING Base Words and Endings with Spelling Changes

If...	a student has difficulty correctly reading base words that have endings with spelling changes,
then...	use Routine 4, Word Parts Strategy, to provide instruction and practice reading the words *panicked, imagining, furious, damaged, replied, panicking, imagined, furiously, replying.*

SUGGESTED SKILL INSTRUCTION If a student scores below 3 for a skill, use the recommendations below to provide additional instruction for the skill.

RATE

If...	a student scores fewer than 120 wpm on this passage,
then...	identify reading rate difficulties (repetitions, ineffective or slow decoding). Help the student correctly read miscues and eliminate repetitions within a paragraph and then reread the paragraph several times. To provide additional practice, use one of the Fluency Routines, 11–14.

ACCURACY

If...	a student's Record of Oral Reading indicates problems decoding specific word types,
then...	analyze the types of miscues made. Have the student reread a sentence with a miscued word. If the student is unable to decode the miscued word, model and teach how to decode those word types. Then have the student read these types of words in continuous texts.

SUMMARIZE

If...	a student is unable to identify important ideas or details in this passage,
then...	model how to identify an important idea and the details that support it as you read aloud part of the passage. Then have the student do the same with the remainder of the passage. Use Routine 16, Summarizing, for additional instruction and practice.

COMPREHENSION Cause and Effect

If...	a student is unable to identify cause and effect in this selection,
then...	have the student identify clue words and phrases that signal cause and effect, such as *so* and *despite*. Then have the student use the Cause and Effect graphic organizer (p. 123) to write a short description of two events in the passage, explaining what happened and why.

VOCABULARY Prefixes and Suffixes *dis-*, *-less*

If...	a student has trouble determining the meanings of words with *-less* or *dis-*,
then...	explain to the student that the prefix *dis-* means "not," or "opposite of," and that the suffix *-less* means "without." Write the following words: *discomfort, powerless, changeless, disallow*. With the student, read each word, determine the meaning, and use it in a sentence.

WORD READING Greek Roots *arch, sy, meter*

If...	a student has difficulty correctly reading words with these Greek roots,
then...	use Routine 4, Word Parts Strategy, to provide instruction and practice reading the words *patriarchs, perimeter, symptoms, architecture, diameter, pedometer, symmetry, system*.

SUGGESTED SKILL INSTRUCTION If a student scores below 3 for a skill, use the recommendations below to provide additional instruction for the skill.

RATE

If...	a student scores fewer than 125 wpm on this passage,
then...	identify reading rate difficulties (repetitions, ineffective or slow decoding). Help the student correctly read miscues and eliminate repetitions within a paragraph and then reread the paragraph several times. To provide additional practice, use one of the Fluency Routines, 11–14.

ACCURACY

If...	a student's Record of Oral Reading indicates problems decoding specific word types,
then...	analyze the types of miscues made. Have the student reread a sentence with a miscued word. If the student is unable to decode the miscued word, model and teach how to decode those word types. Then have the student read these types of words in continuous texts.

RETELL Character, Setting, and Plot

If...	a student is unable to describe the characters, setting, or most important events in the plot,
then...	use the Character, Setting, and Plot graphic organizer (p. 120) or highlight words or phrases in the story to identify information about the characters, setting, or events. Then use Routine 15, Narrative Retelling, to model how to retell the important events in the plot.

COMPREHENSION Draw Conclusions

If...	a student is unable to draw conclusions in this selection,
then...	reread the passage together. Then use the Draw Conclusions graphic organizer (p. 124) to model how to use information from the passage to draw a conclusion about one of the character's feelings and ideas. Work with the student to draw conclusions about another character.

VOCABULARY Roots *archaeo, ped*

If...	a student has trouble identifying the meanings of the words *archaeologists* and *pedometer*,
then...	explain the meanings of the roots *archaeo* (ancient) and *ped* (foot). Work with the student to give a meaning for each of these words and use each in a sentence: *archaeology, biped, pedal, quadraped.*

WORD READING Suffixes *-ive, -ous, -age*

If...	a student has difficulty correctly reading words with these suffixes,
then...	use Routine 4, Word Parts Strategy, to provide instruction and practice reading the words *apprehensive, dangerous, courageous, shortage, adjective, ridiculous, bandage, discourage.*

Moving into Instruction **60**

SUGGESTED SKILL INSTRUCTION If a student scores below 3 for a skill, use the recommendations below to provide additional instruction for the skill.

RATE

If...	a student scores fewer than 120 wpm on this passage,
then...	identify reading rate difficulties (repetitions, ineffective or slow decoding). Help the student correctly read miscues and eliminate repetitions within a paragraph and then reread the paragraph several times. To provide additional practice, use one of the Fluency Routines, 11–14.

ACCURACY

If...	a student's Record of Oral Reading indicates problems decoding specific word types,
then...	analyze the types of miscues made. Have the student reread a sentence with a miscued word. If the student is unable to decode the miscued word, model and teach how to decode those word types. Then have the student read these types of words in continuous texts.

SUMMARIZE

If...	a student is unable to identify important ideas or details in this passage,
then...	model how to identify an important idea and the details that support it as you read aloud part of the passage. Then have the student do the same with the remainder of the passage. Use Routine 16, Summarizing, for additional instruction and practice.

COMPREHENSION Compare and Contrast

If...	a student is unable to identify comparisons and contrasts in this selection,
then...	have the student reread the passage and ask him or her what features described in this passage are being compared and contrasted. Then help the student complete a Venn Diagram graphic organizer (p. 122) to chart similarities and differences between our understanding of volcanoes in the past and now.

VOCABULARY Prefixes and Suffixes *mis-, -ist*

If...	a student has trouble determining the meanings of words with *-ist* or *mis-*,
then...	explain to the student that the prefix *mis-* means "wrongly" and that the suffix *-ist* means "person involved in the activity or field." Write the following words: *misfortune, scientist, misleading, cyclist*. With the student, read each word, determine the meaning, and use it in a sentence.

WORD READING Prefixes *trans-, mis-, pre-*

If...	a student has difficulty correctly reading words with these Greek roots,
then...	use Routine 4, Word Parts Strategy, to provide instruction and practice reading the words *transcribed, precaution, transformed, misunderstood, transportation, preamble, prearrange, miscommunication*.

Moving into Instruction 60

Name _____

SEQUENCE WORDS

_____ _____ _____ _____

_____ _____ _____ _____

1

2

3

4

5

Graphic Organizers

Name _____

CHARACTERS	
Names	Words and Phrases Author Uses to Describe

SETTING	
Place and/or Time	Words and Phrases Author Uses to Describe

PLOT: MAJOR EVENTS
In the beginning...
Next...
After that...
In the end...

Name _____

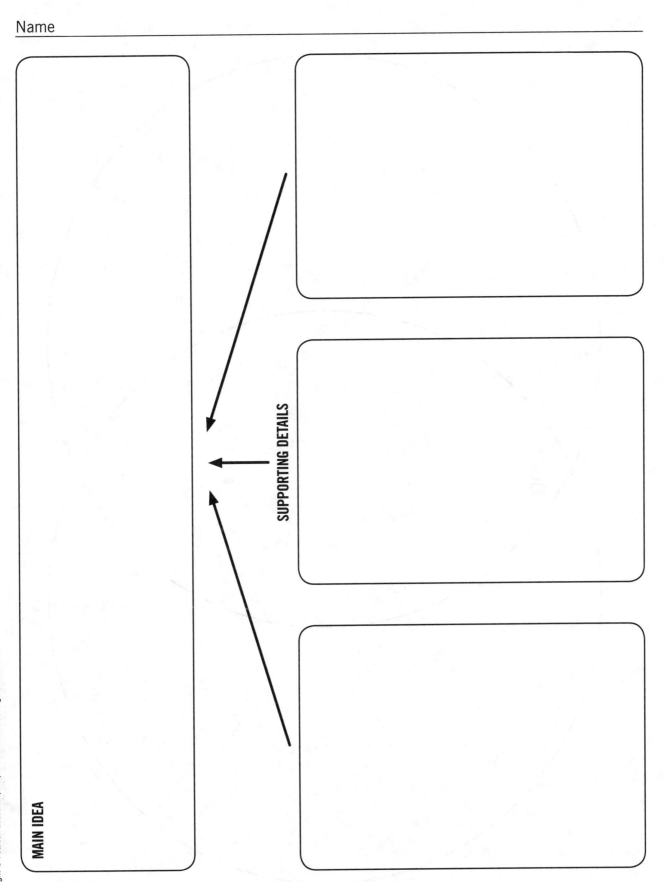

MAIN IDEA

SUPPORTING DETAILS

Name _____

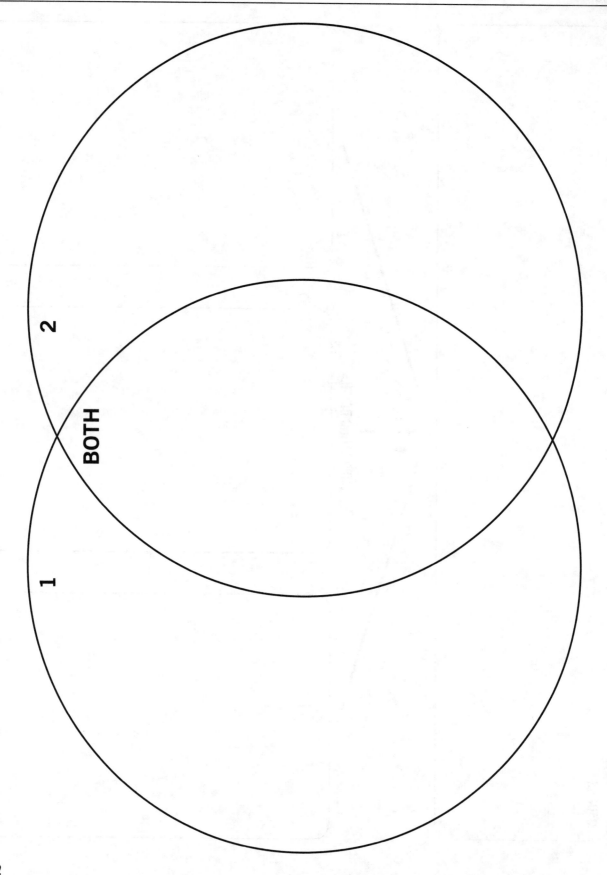

2

BOTH

1

Graphic Organizers

Name

CAUSE

EFFECT

WHY DID IT HAPPEN?

WHAT HAPPENED?

WHY DID IT HAPPEN?

WHAT HAPPENED?

WHY DID IT HAPPEN?

WHAT HAPPENED?

Graphic Organizers

Name

FACTS AND DETAILS

CONCLUSIONS

Name

SCOPE AND SEQUENCE OF SKILLS

Word Reading	4	6	8	10	12	14	16	18	20	24	28	30	34	38	40	50	60
CONSONANTS																	
Final -ck and -ll	1	1															
Blends		1							1	4							
Digraphs				1									1				
Silent Consonants										5							
VOWELS																	
Short Vowels	1	1, 2					1		1		3						
Long Vowels			2						1		3						
r-Controlled Vowels				2					2								
Vowel Digraphs						1	1	4	1							8	
Sounds of y							3										
Diphthongs									5								
Variant Vowels										2		1			1, 7		
WORD STRUCTURE																	
Plural -s	2																
Inflected Endings						2											
Comparative Word Endings								1									
Base Words and Endings			1									3			2	3	12
Contractions					1				4								
Compound Words							2	2		3	2	4					
Syllable Patterns							4		3	1	4	2	4	5	3, 15	4	8
Common Syllables											5		5	3	6, 11	2, 9, 13	3, 10
Prefixes													2		8, 13	10, 12	11, 15
Suffixes													3	4	9, 14	7, 11	5, 14
Greek and Latin Roots															10, 12	6, 14	4, 9, 13
Multisyllabic Words					2							5		1, 2	5	1, 5, 15	1, 2, 7
HIGH-FREQUENCY WORDS								3		1	1				4		

The numbers in the chart refer to the Student Passages in which the skills are assessed.

SCOPE AND SEQUENCE OF SKILLS

Vocabulary	4	6	8	10	12	14	16	18	20	24	28	30	34	38	40	50	60
Concept Words	1,2	2															
Classify and Categorize		1		1													
Antonyms			1	2			1,3		3	5	3	2	5	1			
Synonyms			2			2		3	4	2	2	5		2			
Abbreviations					2												
Context Clues					1		4	1	2,5			3	4	5	4,5,6,8,14,15	1,8,9,12,13	2,4,6,7,11
Multiple-Meaning Words						1		4	1	1	1	1	1	3	1,9,11	4,5,7,15	5,8,9
Compound Words							2	2		3,4		4					3
Prefixes													2		3,7,13	3,10,11	1,13,15
Suffixes											5		2,3	4	3,7,13	3,10,11	1,13,15
Roots															2,10,12	2,6,14	10,12,14

Comprehension	4	6	8	10	12	14	16	18	20	24	28	30	34	38	40	50	60
Character, Setting, and Plot	1,2	1,2	1,2	2	2	2	1,4	1,2	1,3,5	1,3	1,3,5	2,4	1,2,3	1,3	2,4,6,8,10,12,14	1,2,6,8,9,13,14	2,4,6,10,11,12,14
Retelling	1,2	1,2	1,2	2	2	2	1,4	1,2	1,3,5	1,3	1,3,5	2,4	1,2,3	1,3	2,4,6,8,10,12,14	1,2,6,8,9,13,14	2,4,6,10,11,12,14
Main Idea and Details				1	1	1	2,3	3,4	2,4	2,4,5	2,4	1,3,5	4,5	2,4,5	1,3,5,7,9,11,13,15	3,4,5,7,10,11,12,15	1,3,5,7,8,9,13,15
Summarizing				1	1	1	2,3	3,4	2,4	2,4,5	2,4	1,3,5	4,5	2,4,5	1,3,5,7,9,11,13,15	3,4,5,7,10,11,12,15	1,3,5,7,8,9,13,15
Cause and Effect							1,2		4	2,3	4	3	1	3,4	2,8,11	3,9,12	2,8,12,13
Compare and Contrast							4	1,3	1,2	4	5	5		1,5	4,10,13	1,2,6,11	4,10,15
Draw Conclusions						1		2,4	3	5	3	1,2	2,3		1,6,7,12	5,7,8,13,14	5,6,7,9,14
Sequence of Events						2	3		5	1	1,2	4	4,5	2	3,5,9,14,15	4,10,15	1,3,11

The numbers in the chart refer to the Student Passages in which the skills are assessed.